VOICES [illegible]HE
ARAB STREETS

VOICES OF THE ARAB STREETS

Saws and epithets of the Baghdadi street: their place in the colloquial poetry of 'Abbūd al-Karkhī

DR. F.M. CASWELL M.A., D.PHIL.

Matador
9 Priory Business Park,
Wistow Road, Kibworth Beauchamp,
Leicestershire. LE8 0RX
Tel: (+44) 116 279 2299
Fax: (+44) 116 279 2277
Email: books@troubador.co.uk
Web: www.troubador.co.uk/matador

ISBN 978 1780881 584

British Library Cataloguing in Publication Data.
A catalogue record for this book is available from the British Library.

Typeset by Troubador Publishing Ltd, Leicester, UK

Matador is an imprint of Troubador Publishing Ltd

To the memory of Helen

CONTENTS

ACKNOWLEDGMENT

Anyone who attempts an anthology of 'popular' sayings will come up against the difficulty of researching them since, being in the vernacular, they are spoken and rarely written. However, as regards putting together a collection of the saws and aphorisms of the Baghdadi street, Mullā 'Abbūd al-Karkhī is a valuable source. He was born in Baghdad in 1861 and died in 1946. A poet of the common man, using the colloquial Iraqi dialect as his medium, he produced a large volume of poetry, with which he not only regaled his listeners in the weekly radio slots allowed him from time to time – when his acerbic political views were tolerated by the establishment – but also published the poems in a succession of newspapers which were promoted by him and by relatives and friends under his influence. His *Dīwān* was published in four volumes between 1933 and 1938.

Al-Karkhī's *Dīwān* is a historical record in colloquial verse of the political, social and cultural conditions of Iraqi society during the early days of the country's emergence as a state after the First World War – first under British mandate, then as a modern constitutional monarchy which, while it had gained its independence, remained under the tutelage of Britain through a succession of one-sided treaties, against which al-Karkhī was to inveigh time and again. The *Dīwān* is also a treasure house of the Baghdadi language of the street, and of the saws, epithets, proverbs and epigrams used by the common man to express hopes and desires, wants and hardships, criticisms and discontents, the whole distinguishable by being both colloquial and in verse. This is a major source for this book, and my task in incorporating it in the general body of what follows has been made easier by the fact that I was preceded by ‘Azīz Jāsim al-Ḥajjiya, to whom I am greatly indebted; he meticulously went through the *Dīwān*, extracting proverbs and sayings which were then published in their original colloquial Arabic as *al-Amthāl wa l-kināyāt fī shi‘r ‘Abbūd al-Karkhī*, thereby providing me with a ready-made collection of those parts of al-Karkhī’s work that are relevant to my undertaking.

In putting together and listing my choice of the saws and epithets, I have also derived invaluable assistance from some other Arabic collections. Some are very recent, while the scholarly value of all of them is somewhat diminished by being arranged alphabetically rather than by reference to particular topics. I single out in particular the monumental collection of al-Tikrītī’s *Jamharat al-amthāl al-Baghdādiyya* (5,893 *amthāl,* 2,697 pages in five volumes), and the very recent *al-Amthāl al-Baghdādiyya* of Sheikh Jalāl al-Ḥanafī al-Baghdādī.

INTRODUCTION

To a non-Arabist Westerner the epithet 'classical' applied to Arabic would suggest an ancient language as obsolete as, say Greek and Latin. But that would be a misunderstanding. Classical Arabic has its roots in antiquity, but comes down to us largely unchanged as regards grammatical structure, and substantially so as regards vocabulary. A literate person returning to life to-day from pre-Islamic times, and reading an article in, say an Iraqi newspaper written in present-day Classical Arabic, would stumble over a number of words and expressions but would still recognise the writing as being in substantially the same language that was current in his day, and he would also grasp the meaning, albeit with some difficulty. But the endurance of Classical Arabic has not prevented Arab societies from developing their own particular vernacular dialects. Hence one finds in every present-day Arab society two forms of Arabic: 'Classical' – the language of the dictionary – side by side with the demotic vernacular. The corresponding Arabic terms for the two are the *fuṣḥā* and the '*āmmī*; they are distinguishable in several key respects.

The *fuṣḥā* is used in substantially the same form throughout the Arab world. It is the lingua franca of all the Arabs, being also the language of the Koran. The '*āmmī*, on the other hand, is the local language of the state or city. The *fuṣḥā* is both spoken and written. The '*āmmī* is spoken – the language of the home, the street, the market place, and used also by the leaders of society and the literati in everyday discourse. It is rarely found in written form – hence the importance of the contribution made by al-Karkhī in that particular regard. The norm is to speak in *āmmī*, but write in *fuṣḥā*. Thus, as an example, a university professor would discuss the affairs of the day with his colleagues in the common room in *āmmī*, but would use the *fuṣḥā* when writing to his tailor.

As one would expect, the *fuṣḥā* is held in higher esteem than the *āmmī*, which is stigmatised as imperfect Arabic, instead of being accepted as simply a variant form of the same language. Thus we find a prescriptivist like al-Shabībī pointing out that the one thing that all national colloquial versions of the language have in common is the absence of the grammatical suffix (in this case the *ḥaraka* or vowel ending), which, so he asserts, is the touchstone of 'correct' speech.[1] That the *āmmī* is so regarded is implicit in the literal meanings of the two terms: *fuṣḥā* ('eloquent', 'well-spoken'), and *āmmī* ('popular'). A factor in the more exalted position of the *fuṣḥā*, in addition to its being the language of the Koran and thus the devotional language of Islam, lies precisely in the fact that it lends itself to being written, hence standing as a permanent depository of the Arabs' cultural heritage.

The distinction between the *fuṣḥā* and the *āmmī* has far-reaching political and social implications. The *āmmī* can be seen as a national dialect, but only in the sense of local nationality. To an Arab aspiring to make common cause with his Arab brethren everywhere, the *āmmī* is a hindrance, demonstrating the fractures between Arab societies. Thus one finds Aḥmad Bahjat al-Athrī wishing that the *āmmī* be suppressed so as to leave a clear field for the *fuṣḥā* in every Arabic-speaking country, thereby achieving full unity of the 'Arab nation'.[2] Al-Shabībī, for his part, points to the Western

---

[1] al-Shabībī, Sheikh Muḥammad Riḍā, *Mu'jam wa uṣūl al-lahja al-'Irāqiyya*, p. 5.
[2] al-Karkhī, *Dīwān* i, p. 10

Arabists and their Arab counterparts who advocate making the colloquial a subject of formal study; this he dismisses with barely concealed disdain.[3]

> We say that the disappearance of the several versions of the *āmmī* is no loss. What use can there be in a language that is incapable of expressing scientific and literary concepts? Far better to bend our efforts to preserve that which is correct and pure, thereby maintaining its integrity as well as ensuring its common use.

Raphael Baṭṭī goes further:[4] he accuses Western Arabists and Orientalists of having mixed motives in encouraging the study and development of the various forms of the *āmmī* – to wit, a pure, benign and academic interest, intertwined with a desire to obstruct the Arab nation's aspirations to unity. Such aspirations are encouraged by the fact that the *fuṣḥā* is the undisputed official national language of the different Arab states. Another way of stating that fact, again using Iraq as an example, is that the *āmmī* is the language of the Iraqis, while the *fuṣḥā* is the language of Iraq. Thus it is that all acts of state, ordinances, deeds, letters and formal statements are couched in *fuṣḥā*. It is interesting to note that while legal proceedings, including the testimonies of witnesses, the oral submissions of the advocates and even court judgments, are expressed in the vernacular *āmmī*, yet the act of instituting the legal process, all other applications to the court and all written witness statements, as well as the court record (including the formal judgments), are written in *fuṣḥā*. This is also the situation which applies in dealings with other public institutions; thus outside many courthouses and government offices one finds a particular type of scribe

---

[3] al- Shabībī, *Mu'jam*, p. 7.
[4] al-Karkhī, *Dīwān* i, p. 16.

(*ʻarḍiḥālchī*), who offers his services, for payment, to a litigant or petitioner by setting out the client's case in written *fuṣḥā*, which the client then takes into the court or government office to submit as his statement or petition (for it promptly to disappear into the bureaucratic filing system) – even as he is then heard restating his case in his own spoken *āmmī*.

There is also a perception, equally unfair in its general application, that the *āmmī* is a corrupt form of Arabic used by, and for the benefit of, those who are untutored and otherwise endowed with limited education and little ability to use the *fuṣḥā*. One finds an example of this in the patronising words with which the eminent Iraqi poet Maʻrūf al-Ruṣāfī favoured al-Karkhī:[5]

> Our poet al-Karkhī had received a certain measure of education which extended to reading and writing – such that we find a trace of the *fuṣḥā* in his poetry. His spoken verses have greater effect than the written ones, and they tend to jest rather than seriousness. Yet he can have a greater impact on the minds of the populace than those who compose in *fuṣḥā* because he is better understood.

It is to al-Karkhī's credit that he accepted these words in good grace, and had them included as an introduction to his *Dīwān*. Rather than seeing that he was being damned with faint praise, he would have felt flattered by the confirmation of the measure of formal education with which he was endowed, complementing his status as a popular poet who moved the masses, who related to him because he spoke their language. More generously to al-Karkhī, but with no less disdain for the *āmmī*, one finds Fahmī al-Mudarris attributing

[5] Al-Kark*ī*, Dīwān i, p. 21.

the mix of the *āmmī* and the *fuṣḥā* to what he presumes to be al-Karkhī's desire to educate the untutored common man by putting him in touch with the latter.[6] While that is debatable as a general proposition, its opposite rings more true. There is little doubt that al-Karkhī was preoccupied with introducing the tutored to his *āmmī*, which he published in a succession of newspapers (as one after another they suffered closure by the authorities). In that respect – i.e. in committing *āmmī* poetry to the printed page, so as to popularise it as a medium accessible to the better-educated – there are serious obstacles to surmount. For a start there is the representation in the spoken Baghdadi dialect of certain orthographic characters by sounds popularly considered 'harsher' than those used in other dialects (with the 'ch' being ubiquitous); thus:

s pronounced as ṣ (as in faraṣ for faras)

dh pronounced as ḍ (as in ḍāg for dhāq)

k pronounced as ch (as in *chāna* for *kāna*; *ḥichāya* for *ḥikāya*; *dīch* for *dīk*)

q pronounced as g (as in *galb* for *qalb*); as j (as in *juddām* for *quddām*; *ḥarīj* for *ḥarīq*); or as k (as in *wakit* for *waqt*)

There is also the widespread use of words imported from other languages, of which one can identify Persian, Turkish, English and Hindi, a testament to the nations that have invaded Iraq at different times, as well as a smattering of Kurdish, Baghdadi Judeo-Arabic and French. The purist may characterise them as foreign intrusions, tending to

[6] Al-Karkhī, *Dīwān* i, p. 13.

corruption and abomination;[7] but to al-Karkhī they were integral to his Baghdadi *'āmmī*. His principal concession to the *fuṣḥā* can be said to consist of the inclusion in his *Dīwān* of Classical Arabic words that are otherwise alien to the common *āmmī*, such as *fī*, *immā*, *ayna*, *ayyuha*, *limādha*, *kadhālika*. Another concession to the *fuṣḥā* is his occasional addition of the (*ḥarakāt*) vowels to word endings.

Al-Karkhī's verses are generally regarded as being more in jest than seriousness. But that is very wide of the mark. That they were in the demotic *āmmī* would have made them appear comic, but this disguised a serious intent. Al-Karkhī was a political animal, a social reformer verging on the revolutionary, a fervent Iraqi nationalist, a literary scourge of all those he perceived as foreign intruders – Johnny-come-lately exploiters – into Iraqi public life. He was a master of invective, immodestly comparing himself to the great mediaeval satirist Jarīr. But while Jarīr's acerbic verses scandalised a whole society, al-Karkhī always had his artillery trained on the high and mighty. He was acutely conscious of Western political influences, as well as new fashions in dress, drink and food to which traditional Iraqi society had become exposed after the First World War. A constant theme in his poetry was a call to resist foreign occupation and foreign influences, to excoriate those of his own people who served the interests of the occupier, to repudiate sectarianism, and most of all to denounce corruption and hypocrisy in public life. The comic element served as a cover – it made him appear less threatening. Author of

> You feeble-minded people, you curs
> living as captives ruled by women

---

[7] al-Shabībī, *Mu'jam*, p. 10.

alluding in 'ruled by women' to Gertrude Bell – British Oriental Commissioner and intimate of King Faiṣal the First – he was still received regularly in the palace to entertain the king with his racy colloquial poetry from the Baghdadi tea-houses. As he buttonholed the Minister of the Interior to complain about repressive media censorship, the latter (who boasted a Parisian Left Bank education) could playfully shrug off the criticism of the versifier from the Karkh quarter of Baghdad with the words: 'We only passed the law because of your *chantage*!' When the word *chantage* was later inaccurately explained to al-Karkhī – he took it to mean that he was being accused of subversion – he proudly declared: '*chantage* for ever!' – ('blackmail and extortion for ever!').

THE DĪWĀN

The *Dīwān* is arranged in separate sections: social affairs, politics, questions of journalism, criticism and satire, eroticism and miscellany. But the arrangement is a mere editorial contrivance; the bulk of the work saw the light of day as leading articles that appeared over the years under the name of al-Karkhī in the dozen or so newspapers published by him, or his close relatives and associates. The distinctive features of the articles is that they are entirely in verse, and use the *'āmmī* or Baghdadi vernacular. While politics, under which the travails of journalism can be taken as subsumed, accounts for some two-thirds of the total, one may perhaps consider the rest to be more valuable as a social record of the conditions and concerns of the Iraqi peoples during a critical historical period – following the First World War, and with it the end of four centuries of Ottoman rule, followed by British occupation and then by the installation of a constitutional monarchy under British tutelage. Another discernible feature in this social record is that it deals with ordinary, everyday topics, often based on the personal experience of the author. There is the occasion when we find him regretting (tongue in cheek) having taken a train instead of undertaking the journey on the back of a camel: engine slow as a beetle proceeding the whole night and most of the following day in a dignified, unhurried manner to cover the distance from Baghdad to Kirkuk; hard seating fit only for stoics; absence of food and refreshments other than tepid water; loss or theft of a rug in the night, a report of which is met by shrugged shoulders. On other occasions one finds the author bemoaning a venture into farming, which ended disastrously with the collapse of world cereal prices, exacerbated in his particular case by the theft of his cows, for which he got no redress from either the local constabulary or the judiciary. He criticises a host who entertains him to a dinner of chicken, but who then spends the rest of the evening lauding its superior qualities. He excoriates the guests at wedding receptions who bring along uninvited children, whose strident noise and mischief spoil the guests' enjoyment. He takes to task those of his subscribers who delay payment, and who ignore reminders. He congratulates himself on the successful defence of a libel action brought by a Christian in respect of a scurrilous poem mocking Christian ways and habits, and then proceeds to celebrate the acquittal by adding further defamation to the original. He answers anonymous complaints by heaping disgrace and dishonour on their writer, whom he challenges to come out into the open. He mildly curses a friend who took away his spectacles to have them repaired but failed to return them as promised, and goes on to threaten worse curses and more if the man delayed any further. In a more lofty tone he addresses the evils of drink, betting on horses, ram and cockfighting, smoking, as well as tea-drinking, which last had begun to be very popular in the 1920s.

Al-Karkhī's political output was conditioned by the Shī'ite uprising against British rule in the 1920s; and for the rest of his life he did not veer from his opposition to foreign occupation and imperialist exploitation. Primary targets of his vitriol were also corruption in high places and betrayal by those who, in return for preferment and monetary reward, served the interests of foreigners rather than their own people. Yet a remarkable aspect of his political satire is the degree with which it was tolerated by the authorities. Whenever he was seen to have stepped immoderately out of line – as by going too far in his attack on a minister or, as was often the case, on the perennial prime minister Nūrī al-Sa'īd – his newspaper would be closed and its licence revoked. But that would be followed soon after by a new licence for a new title being granted to him or to an associate; he was made to suffer financial loss without being silenced as a journalist and critic. One explanation for this qualified toleration is the protection he had from Faiṣal I and his successor Ghāzī. They were a Hashemite family from Hijaz, brought to Iraq after failing to gain the throne of Syria, and then installed as a new Iraqi monarchy with the support and under the aegis of Britain, and in the face of substantial local opposition. More generally, Faiṣal was a Sunni and the Shī'a resented his instalment as king, which they took to signal their subjugation by the British to the Sunni minority. It would have suited the palace to have a popular voice publicly declare his respect and fealty to it, even while excoriating the imperial power behind it. That said, there is cogent evidence that Faiṣal was genuinely fond of al-Karkhī, and liked to be entertained by him.

But that was not the full explanation for the indulgence shown to him. That his political pronouncements were of a subversive nature was all too evident, but his subversion was of a special and engaging kind which would have been seen primarily as bold and irreverent mischief embodied in the semi-comic language of a *shuway'ir* ('poetaster'), evoking more mirth than insurgency. He was allowed a weekly 15-minute slot on the radio (then a novelty), at times extended to half an hour. His broadcasts were censored to the extent that he had to submit the material beforehand to the authorities for approval. On one occasion, as soon as he began the broadcast, he laid aside the approved text, took a substitute from his pocket and began to read it. The broadcast was cut off by the monitor, and this was followed by the announcement that the interruption was due to technical reasons – an explanation that would hardly have fooled the regular listeners in the tea houses. They would have smiled as they had it confirmed to them that the Mullā of the Karkh was his mischievous self again.

Al-Karkhī liked to convey his political message by the use of fables, some lifted straight out of La Fontaine: the fox and the cockerel, the cat and the mouse, the wolf and the lamb – in each case the strong and crafty aggressor standing for the imperial power, the weak and ingenuous for the Iraqi people. He would then add disingenuously:

I have foresworn frank talk and too much disclosure
I have become a composer of verses and fables
So I can make the verse as one covered in spots
soft to the touch – dread its bite

and also declaring mischievously: 'We have forsworn the truth, all we want is our livelihood' – a variation of his oft used epithet: 'We have given up on the dates, all we want is our basket!'

Al-Karkhī is widely viewed, above all else, as an Iraqi and Arab nationalist. He himself would not have dissented from that view. But his is a particular form of nationalism, which often descends to xenophobia. To him the British government is a far-away shadowy *Thamesī* quietly plotting and manipulating and sending its agents to further its worldwide interests. But the author is not concerned to examine and discuss such abstract concepts as imperialism, colonialism and nationalism, nor to address on an ideological level the intricacies of economic exploitation. The furthest he strays in that direction is to complain at the occupying power encouraging the importation and consumption of tea in the 1920s, to the detriment of the market in dates, in which he dabbled for a time, and their derivative date wine. His real concern, typically down-to-earth, is with the outsiders whom he calls *dukhalā'* ('intruders' – 'they are the greatest calamity') whom he takes to be the individual advisers and bureaucrats: the Mr Cook accused of stealing and carrying away national antiques, the Mr Baker evading payment of what was due to the municipality, the Indian bureaucrat Cafāyāt extorting fortunes which he gambles away on the card tables, and inspector Azdū, a typical foreign railway employee whose rudeness to and humiliation of the passengers are observed by al-Karkhī at close quarters. And his concerns are also focused on others who entered his society under the aegis of the *Thamesī* to turn things upside down, as they wrested centre stage from the indigenous Iraqi:

> In my household the Armenian has become a Qaḥṭānī
> while your humble servant is reduced to a Greek
> A Ḥimyarī the Indian, and I a German
> you might as well say my granddad was born a Rumanian

Among the *dukhalā'*, his *bêtes noires* are the Assyrians or Nestorians, Christian refugees from the Ottoman Empire who entered Iraq following the British occupation, were enlisted in British service and were given a leading position in the running of the railways ('half-owned by the Assyrians, the other half by the Armenians'). In that respect al-Karkhī may be seen, to his discredit, joining the whipping up of atavistic popular feelings against the Nestorians, culminating in communal violence, brutal intervention by army and air force, and much shedding of blood.[8] As an example of foreign companies damaging traditional local crafts he singles out the Czechoslovak company Bata, manufacturer and retailer of footwear:

> They took over commerce
> and monopolised industry
> They filled the jobs
> and pushed and shoved and ruled

[8] A graphic description of the massacre can be found in Robert Byron's *The Road to Oxiana*, p. 46.

A darker side to that nationalism, or rather xenophobia, is that al-Karkhī often includes in the class of *dukhalā'* members of ethnic minorities which had inhabited Iraq for centuries, albeit at the outer edge of a mainly Arab society, but who were now perceived to be benefiting from the disappearance of the rigid Ottoman *millet* system and its replacement by a Western liberal regime that recognised no sectarian divisions or constraints:

> Would you compare Ibn 'Abdaka[9] with Murdokh and Shā'ūl,
> measure the noble steeds against the asses?

and

> The Times have made me a captive
> of Moshi and Ezra and a curry-eating Indian

Next to hatred of foreigners one finds the author expressing his dislike of non-Iraqi Arab entertainers, including the celebrated Egyptian singers 'Abd al-Wahhāb and Umm Kalthūm, as well as theatrical entertainers such as the circus company of Yūsuf Wahbī, whom he sees as Johnny-come-latelies amassing fortunes and supplanting local talent in popular esteem:

> He has gone Abū Jāsim
> al-Wahbī now in his place
> Gone, gone for ever our Abū Jāsim
> to Allāh raising his plea
> Recitor of 'Yā jārata l-wādī'
> that moved the very beetle to rapture

---

[9] A celebrated 'noble' outlaw, who later in life joined the insurgency against British occupation in the 1920s; see 'Abd al-Karim al-'Allāf, *Baghdād al-qadīma*, p. 145; Matthew Caswell, *Menashi's Boy*, p. 21. Murdokh and Shā'ūl are common names for a Christian and a Jew respectively.

A man with an acute social conscience, there is no levity in al-Karkhī's epic "al-Majrasha"('the quern') in which are described the hardships in the life of the poor, oppressed, hard-working Iraqi woman and wife. It is a long poem, which would hardly suffer if reduced to one-third of its length – al-Karkhī is notorious for his prolixity and for gilding the metaphorical lily. A hallmark of his style is the juxtaposition of opposites e.g. 'The Times have become as molasses and cream with the ignoble/while serving the cup of bitterness to the noble'. But where one or two metaphors might be seen as adequate to make the point he cannot resist using a host of them.

The poem sets the scene with a woman at the quern bemoaning her ill-fortune – enslaved to repetitive, arduous work, to unremitting misery and deprivation, and to a cruel and repulsive master and man. The poem opens with a couplet:

> I gave up my soul to hand-milling
> and know that hand-milling is bad for it
> Soon I shall smash the quern
> and curse all that promote it

This is followed by 72 quatrains, the first hemistich of the first verse of each quatrain starting with 'Soon I shall smash the quern'.

The woman may perhaps be identified as a member of the semi-tribal community of *mu'dān* (water-buffalo keepers, vendors of milk and clotted cream) inhabiting the predominantly Shī'ite district south of Baghdad, with Ḥilla at its centre and close to the holy shrines of Karbala and Najaf. More precisely, we may take it that 'Afjar is her native village. It is worth noting that the author's own family hailed from that area – as he would be reminded from time to time by those, somewhat ill-disposed towards him, who referred to him as al-Ḥillāwī. His reaction to this was to abjure the sectarianism implicit in the Ḥillī association, while asserting his non-sectarian Iraqi nationalism, as well as his close identification with the Karkh Bank of Baghdad.

Time and again the woman refers to the man in the poem as 'my master'. He is most disagreeable, so old and decrepit he could be taken to be a contemporary of Noah – stooped, hobbling on creaking knee joints, black as a black slave, dirty, toothless, his eyes filmed with white, and with a spiky bush for a beard. He is cruel, screaming at her for the least transgression and beating her for the smallest provocation, or none. He makes her work at the quern from dusk till dawn, in return for a *qrān*;[10] screaming obscenities while pulling her hair if ever she slackened. One might have expected the author to refer to the woman as working from dawn till dusk; but one can exclude the possibility of an unintended slip: the same expression, 'from dusk till dawn', is repeated more than once. It is only as the woman nears the end of the poem that 'master' becomes 'my old man', as she curses him. In the meantime one hears her bitterly blaming her mother for getting her involved with him, wishing mother and father blind for not seeing what they had brought her to ('a child wedded to a repulsive man so old that he remembers the digging of the sea'), and criticising uncles and tribe for abandoning her. And all the time the man is standing over her as she works the quern, saying: 'She is my slave, I bought her in the market' – which may be taken as an allusion to the bride money.

The poem then moves to another theme, which accounts for the major part of its length. The fault is not simply in father,

---

[10] The *qrān* is 20 *fils*; there are 1,000 *fil*s to a *dīnār*.

mother, uncles and tribe that the woman is enslaved, condemned to the quern from dusk till dawn; rather, the fault is in a perverse fate that condemns the good as it rewards the unworthy:

> The daughter of the noble tribes and Arabs is given to the scoundrel
> while the daughter of the rogue is indulged by a sheikh

and

> O Thou Creator of all
> who oversaw the loading of Noah's ark
> Can it be right that I daughter of 'Usayla[11] be mated to a scurvy nag?

The fortunate woman living in the lap of luxury and ease ('reclining in shiny bracelets and bangles') is identified as a modern woman who emulates the *franjiyya* (Western women), who wears a suit and a hat, uses make-up, manicures her nails and bares her arms in public. That leads to another important and final theme: there are changes afoot; the social fabric is shaken; the centre cannot hold; certainty gives way to disorder:

> Time has confused your world
> confusion, utter confusion
> The bald woman and the one with tresses
> Allāh has caused them to be equal

Those who were ahead are now overtaken by those who were behind; things cannot be allowed to remain as they are; worse may follow. A radical remedy is called for before it is too late – in other words, it is time to smash the quern.

---

[11] A celebrated race-horse in the 1930s.

And then what? In desperation the woman ponders whether it might not be better for her to tread the European path:

> Soon I shall smash the quern
> to Austria and Hungary wend my way
> There to abjure the lot of them
> Tubba', Qaḥṭān, al-Ṭā'ī and Mudhar[12]

But the reader is left in no doubt what she would really rather do once her freedom is attained: not follow modern Western innovations, comfortable though they are, but return to her roots – through al-Ṣīra, al-Hindiyya, al-Karrādī, Shaṭra, and a score of other native localities on the way back – to rediscover herself as she invokes the protection and help of the 'honourable sheikhs of the Arabs'. This reflects al-Karkhī's stance in the face of the changes that were happening all around him, and can be seen as the foundation of his xenophobia. At the same time it may explain the attraction that his brand of poetry held for Faiṣal – a prince of Hijaz, who had exchanged his tribal tented *muḍīf* ('reception hall') for a royal palace in Baghdad, while remaining at heart a traditional tribal chieftain. Besides, Faiṣal would see himself as one of the 'honourable sheikhs of the Arabs' whose protection the woman at the quern invokes, and is identified as such in the poem's concluding quatrain:

> Soon I shall smash the quern
> then exhausted trudge the night away
> To Baghdad and al-Karkhī to moan
> of hardship, sleeplessness, hunger and thirst complain
> So he'll write it in "*al-Karkh*"
> and repeat it to the King

---

[12] Tribal names.

However, al-Karkhī's romanticism is tempered by realism. Had he not gone and seen with his own eyes in the cities and villages across Iraq – Basra, Samarra, Jassān and many others – their prevailing dirt, squalor, ignorance and disorder? Did he not time and again inveigh against their backwardness, meanness and ignorance? In comparison, he could not help but respect the vigour and technological advances of the West as he exhorts his people to emulate its industry and its combination of power and knowledge: knowledge without power will not avail, while power without knowledge is not worth twopence. At the same time, al-Karkhī sees neighbouring Turkey and Iran undergo a serious political and cultural lurch towards secularism and Western ways. Further, al-Karkhī lived long enough to survive the Second World War. In the decade preceding it, and in the course of it, he saw his country become a battle ground in which opposing European powers and ideologies vied with each other, while the daily war-news bulletins demonstrated the might and technological superiority of Western man and the vast gulf between him and the poet's own people:

> You produce the earthen oven
> and from the fronds of date trees the broom and the basket
> He manufactures guns and submarines
> machine guns and airplanes

And so one finds al-Karkhī towards the end of his life surrendering by and by to the inevitable; let's turn our back on the past and be the children of the hour, he is heard to declare, as he symbolically exchanges the traditional Arab dress for a suit and a *sidāra*.[13]

---

[13] A rimless felt hat popularised by Faiṣal.

BIBLIOGRAPHY

al-'Allāf, 'Abd al-Karīm, *Baghdad al-qadīma*. Beirut: al-Dār al-'arabiyya li l-mawsū'āt, 1999.

Byron, Robert, *The Road to Oxiana*. London: Cape, 1937.

Caswell, Matthew, 'The life and death of a brigand', in *Menashi's Boy*. Leicester: Matador, 2010.

al-Ḥajjiya, 'Azīz Jāsim, *al-Amthāl wa l-kināyāt fī shi'r 'Abbūd al-Karkhī*. Baghdad: Maktabat al-nahḍa l-'arabiyya, 1986.

al-Ḥanafī al-Baghdādī, al-Sheikh Jalāl, *al-Amthāl al-Baghdādiyya*. Beirut: al-Dār al-'arabiyya li l-mawsū'āt, 2011.

al-Karkhī, *Dīwān*, vols. I-III. Baghdad: Maṭba'at al-ma'ārif, 1956–67.

—— vol. IV. Baghdad: Maktabat al-nahḍa al-'arabiyya, 1987.

Muḥammad, Zāhid, *Dirāsāt 'an al-Mullā 'Abbūd al-Karkhī*. Baghdad: Dār al-ḥurriya li l-ṭibā'a, 1971.

al-Shabībī, Sheikh Muḥammad Riḍā, *Mu'jam wa uṣūl al-lahja al-'Irāqiyya*. Beirut: Dār al-'arabiyya li l-mawsū'āt, 2007.

al-Shālchī, 'Abbūd, *al-kināyāt al-'āmiyya al-Baghdādiyya*. Beirut: Maṭba'at dār al-ṣadir, 1979.

—— *Mawsū'āt l-kināyāt al-Baghdādiyya,* vols. I-III. Beirut: Maṭba'at dār al-kutub, 1982–83.

al-Tikrītī, 'Abd al-Raḥmān, *Jamharat al-amthāl al-Baghdādiyya*, vols I–V. Baghdad: Maṭba'at al-irshād, 1971–81.

SAWS AND EPITHETS

Acknowledgment
Addiction
Allusion
Altruism
Anxiety
Arrogance
Avarice
Bad temper
Baseness
Boasting
Bores
Breeding
Business
Calamity
Caution
Certainty
Charlatanism
Comeuppance
Compatibility
Contentment
Corruption
Crisis
Criticism
Cruelty
Cynicism
Decorum
Despair
Discord
Dishonesty
Dishonour
Disloyalty
Disorder
Doubt
Eyes
Experience
Exaggeration
Exploitation
Extremism
Flattery
Fortune
Friendship
Futility
Feud
Garrulity
Generosity
Good Fortune
Greed
Hardship
Health
Heart
Hospitality
Humiliation
Hypocrisy
Impassivity
Indolence
Ingratitude
Irony
Justice
Khashm
Kinship
Marriage
Meddling
Moderation
Moustaches
Neighbours
Notoriety
Obstinacy
Old age
Parasites
Patience
Praiseworthiness
Profession
Provocation
Quandary
Reconciliation
Resignation
Salvation
Sarcasm
Self-reliance
Stupidity
Superstition
The English
The Table
Teachers

Thrift
Treachery
Uncertainty
Vicissitudes
Weather
Wellbeing
Wisdom
Women

The quotations are from the *Dīwān*, translated by the present author.

SAWS AND EPITHETS

Acknowledgement

Remember the bread and salt.

> Food (bread and salt) is offered by way of hospitality, and in receiving it the guest is taken to be implicitly pledging to honour his friendship and loyalty. To abuse it is the height of disgrace.
>
> Anecdote: a burglar entered a house and found a substance like powder in a tin. He put a pinch on his tongue and found it was salt. He went out and told his lookout that he could not continue with their dishonest enterprise because he had accepted the householder's salt.

This is not the horse's house.

> This is an allusion to the game of chess: the knight does not go there, meaning that the act or omission complained of is improper.

When he was alive they did not clothe him in a *jubba.*[14] When he died they built him a shrine.

When the elephant dies its bones become a souvenir.

---

[14] A cloak denoting a cleric.

When a man dies his legs become longer.

He acquires more respect.

Like the fish, eaten and blamed.

While being consumed, it is blamed for containing bones, and if it was less than fresh probably also for causing an upset stomach.

Nobody really knows you, O *leben*,[15] except the one who mixed you.

A pearl in the hand of a coal merchant.

I nourished him with loads of meat.

The inference is that the recipient abused the munificence of the speaker.

Quarters and halves of meat I gave him to eat
and raised the vain one over all his peers
Taught him rhymes and poetry read to him
and perversely His Excellency mistreated me to unbelief

You will only know my virtue after you have tried others.

The animal is recognised by its dung.

Food in the mouth of the man is religion; in the mouth of the ingrate it is alms.

When you have it in your hand, its charm flees.

[15] A yoghurt drink.

Addiction

Not giving up the wine while there are dates on the trees.

The allusion is to date wine.

It's Satan that whispered in his ear.

A screw in the brain.

There's a voice in the head.

Do not wish the drunkard to fall – he will fall by himself.

What can we do with you, Mullā Ḥammādī?

Allusion

I tell it to you, my daughter, but overhear it, daughter-in-law.

Conveying a criticism or complaint indirectly.

I mean you, but let the neighbour overhear.

To teach the bride, beat the cat.

He who knows knows, but to him who does not know it's a handful of lentils.

This is readily recognisable to Baghdadis as referring to a popular story or theme with variations, the following being one such. A man goes home and finds his wife in a compromising situation with a stranger; the latter runs away and the husband gives chase. Traversing the market, the stranger picks a handful of lentils displayed for sale in an open pannier, and continues to run, pursued by the husband. The onlookers reproach the husband for making such a fuss over a mere handful of lentils. The husband, ashamed to tell the truth, replies as above.

To the free man a sign is enough.

The distant one (*al-ba'īd*), or (more explicitly) *al-ba'īd 'annak* (the one distant from you).

This alludes to a hypothetical unknown to whom is ascribed the gross vice or other disgraceful trait mentioned in the conversation. By using *al-ba'īd* the interlocutor puts a distance between the one with the vice and the listener.

After we had spent five years in Journalism
some good people invested in us
While the misers gave us a wide berth
as if we were some (*al-ba'īd*) dirty pimps

Not for the love of Moses but to spite Pharaoh.

He does not lament Hussain, he laments the stew.

Altruism

Like the candle that burns itself while illuminating others.

No load will be left fallen on the road.

Bystanders will help pick it up, as a good turn.

To every crisis there's an end.

A *Ḥajjī Buktāsh* carrying the *qazān* ('cauldron').

> The Buktāchīs were a religious sect who took part in the ceremonial serving of food to the Ottoman army. The *qazān* (cauldron) was the centrepiece of the ceremony in every unit. It contained the food served out to the soldiers as they queued to receive it, each of them expressing his thanks by raising his hand to his forehead and affirming his fealty by such words as 'May Allāh grant victory to the Sultan'. An army mutiny would usually be signalled by the overturning of the *qazān*.

The silk worm gives silk and dies in the process.

Like the needle, clothing others while it is naked.

Lucifer carrying the burden of Adam and his descendants.

His property is for others.

The drum in his lap, but the stick is in the hand of another.

If he thought he was any good he would have played for himself.

Anxiety

A mother lost her child.

Like a bird that's lost its home.

Approach what you fear, then feel safe.

The house is small and the mules are agitated.

A daughter would be an anxiety even if she were the Virgin Mary.

Rather a beaker of poison than a *mithqāl*[16] of worry.

In his anxiety he sold the camel for the price of its load.

Close the door and be relieved of the troublesome wind.

The date tree says: keep my sister at a distance from me so she does not get on my nerves.

Enough to turn the suckling child grey.

Arrogance

A peacock boasting prettily, as if worth the two banks.

> Baghdad's two banks, the Ruṣāfa and the Karkh – hence the whole of Baghdad.

If God wants to devastate the ant, He gives it wings.

The jackal is belted in the belt of the lion.

The jackal has become a *sayyid.*[17]

For want of steeds they saddled dogs.

He presents himself to me as *glāwāt.*

---

[16] A unit of weight, 3.64 grams, used in jewellery.

[17] A gentleman; in the right context a descendant member of the house of the Prophet.

The *klāwāt* (pronounced '*glāwāt*' by Baghdadis) were the headgear of an officer in the Ottoman army.

The higher the bird soars, just so the further it falls.

Just as you blow, so you'll subside.

They bring the black one[18] to be shod, and the beetle lifts its foot.

For the camel to see its hump it'll have its neck broken.

If I were a prince and you were a prince, who then would drive the donkeys?

To me a lion, but in war a peahen.

My father only has the measure of my mother.

A big and empty drum.

Rags dressed up as silk.

He aspires to the throne even if it's made of bricks.

He thinks death has nodded.

Tomorrow a span and four fingers.

> Your love has lit live coals in my heart
>   douse it may your life be cut short
> Do you not fear the grave
>   tomorrow a span and four fingers

---

[18] A horse.

The camel is also big.

Pocket empty and nose in the air.

Get yourself a tomb before tombs become scarce.

Death does not discriminate.

He greets you praising himself.

Avarice

Generosity is a day, avarice an eternity.

The dead of the graves.

> You cannot get anything from them.

His pocket is guarded by a talisman.

The house is yours but the mosque is nearer/warmer.

> You are welcome to our house as a guest but you would find the mosque more congenial.

A hair from the skin of a pig.

> The allusion is to the difficulty of getting anything from the person so described.

There's no fat in a dog's tail.

Made him a 'Qarandal'.[19]

[19] An assumed name for a simpleton.

An allusion to a fuller version: Qarandal was kept awake when pies were being made (so that he would help in the work), but his sleep was left undisturbed when it was time to consume them.

His smoke blinded me, and I did not get a morsel of the food.

There is no oil in broad beans.

They feel a request like a needle stuck in their flesh.

You might as well squeeze oil out of chaff.

If he has more soup than he needs he would rather leave it on his shirt.

Like Ibn Dalla.

The nickname of ʻAbd al-Qādir Dalla, famous for great wealth and extreme avarice. He founded the bazaar known as Khān Dalla.

There are no pockets in a shroud.

If coffins could be had for free, everyone would want to die.

The dog of the orchard; he neither eats nor lets others eat.

As a general custom, it is permissible for a guest, or even a 'well-intentioned' trespasser (a presumed licensee) in an orchard to pick and eat fruit on site; but not to take any away.

To the avaricious, free vinegar is sweeter than honey.

More avaricious than the winter night.

> Such that one would not venture out of doors and incur an expense.

He would not even piss on a cut hand.

> Based on the belief that urine on a wound will prevent infection and act as a curative.

A tree that provides no shade is worthy to be cut.

Me and not the red ones.

> This is understood as referring to an anecdote demonstrating the meanness of the Bedouins: a certain Bedouin who normally went about in his bare feet, as Beduoins normally do, was the proud owner of a red pair of shoes which he would only wear on the odd occasions when he came to Baghdad on business. On the way he would carry them in his pocket and get them out to put on as he came to the pontoon bridge over the Tigris leading to the market place. On one such occasion, as it was raining, he decided to put off wearing the shoes so as to spare them until he got to the other end of the bridge. As he went across he did not notice a protruding nail which went through his foot. The Bedouin, in the words above, is thanking providence that it had fortuitously occurred to him to put off wearing the 'red ones'.

An egg in the hand of an orphan.

The wealth of the avaricious belongs to Iblīs (Lucifer).

Bad temper

A sour piss.

The vinegar does not respect its container.

A hot head.

A dispute over a blanket.

If everyone was a fire, the world would be consumed by the flames.

The bad-tempered hits the wall with his head.

The plate is hotter than the food.

Treat him with delicacy; cook a meal and invite him.

A *m'aydī*[20] buying mischief.

Beware the one who is taciturn; have no concerns about the bad-tempered.

He will soon calm down.

The pan's on fire!

Breaking the water melon and scattering the seeds.

Shut up, or I'll smash the jar.

Tongue as a saw.

---

[20] One of the water-buffalo keepers who inhabit the marshlands of southern Iraq.

Ten fights an hour.

The snake is not killed by its venom.

Abū Jāsim, a dagger in his belt.

Baseness

Ḥaṭḥūṭ

> A base man. The origin of the word is *ḥaṭṭa*, 'he is fallen'; the *ḥaṭḥūṭ* invests it with onomatopoeic effect.

A black spotted snake.

Backward like the peeing of a camel.

Like the bricks of the privy, each worse than its neighbour/the one underneath it.

To the scorpion, the shoe.

The rotten carcass does not sink.

A *sayyid*, rotten carcass his grandfather.

> Pretending to be of noble lineage whereas he is descended from a base family.

The saline (soil) is no good.

The professional mourner (*'addāda*)[21] will have a job thinking what to say.

---

[21] Professional mourner (female): literally 'the one who reckons' i.e. enumerates the virtues of the departed.

Like a bald chicken.

Like a wet dog.[22]

No matter how fat the dog gets, it is still inedible.

Take the water tank[23] and follow them.

> The reference is to a lowly man who would follow the caravan in the hope of getting some benefit.

He has no capital with anyone.

> He has not acquired a store of others' goodwill and regard through good deeds.

Like a monkey's arse.

> If you give it a coin it will put its hand on its head; but if you give it nothing, it shows you its posterior.

You need to use dirt to remove dirt.

You need a bent stick to clear a bent pipe.

He did a sale and a clearance.

> Lost all sense of shame.

Death veils all faults.

---

[22] Dogs are generally despised by Arabs, and a wet dog doubly so, as it wets those close to it as it shakes itself dry.

[23] The word actually used, *tanka*, is derived from the English 'tin can' or tank.

The *khashm* of the boot.

> The term *khashm* ('nose') has important connotations in the colloquial Baghdadi dialect: it represents pride and manhood. One would metaphorically dismiss an adversary/adversary's argument with the *khashm* (toe) of one's boot. And see ***Khashm*** further down.

A follower of the *mu'dān.*[24]

His word is no better than his piss.

The wretched die wretched.

A dog is a dog even when you put a gold collar on it.

Worse than the *yemenī.*

> The word *yemenī* refers to 'slippers' in the Baghdadi dialect, the origin being footwear imported from Yemen.

He washes his face with his own urine.

Boasting

A big and empty drum.

He only has air in his knapsack.

Woe to it, the *bāmya* (okra), it distends the stomach.

To me a lion but in wars an ostrich/a peahen.

---

[24] See note 20.

In war, a gazelle in flight.

The king is not his uncle.

(Boasting of) a better lineage than the king's.

They asked the mule: Who is your father? It replied: The horse is my uncle.

Nose high in the air.

He holds his nose high in the air
as if he had lent a million to his Lord

Not everyone covered in soot can claim to be a blacksmith.

He who boasts about his health will fall ill; and he who boasts about his wealth will lose it.

Have you heard the news? Praise be to God, the mother of the girls has given birth to a boy!

Said sarcastically.

Bores/unwanted guests

His day is a month, his month a year, his year an age, his age an eternity.

Colder than ice.

Colder than the bottom of the *ḥubb*.[25]

[25] An earthenware water container with a wide opening at the top and tapering down to a pointed base, dripping cool water into a receptacle.

More tiresome than a chaperone.

Heavier than the drain cover.

The fly is not dirty but vexatious.

Heavy on the stomach.

One cannot swallow him even if laced with honey/or sugar.

His being near is grief, his absence a holiday.

An unwelcome guest overstays his welcome like the British Empire.

Put him in a holed *quffa*[26] and cast him off on the river.

Send him on a journey from which there is no return.

A neighbour in a white chemise.

> The reference is to a neighbour in her nightdress who engages one at the end of the day in an interminable boring conversation.

A guest planting a date tree sapling.

> It would take the sapling upwards of 20 years to grow to full maturity.

A tale of the snake/the Sultans.

---

[26] A river craft that has plied the river Tigris from time immemorial. It is completely circular, made of wooden spines covered in skins. It is propelled in a circular motion by the use of an oar.

Never-ending.

Longer than a night of hunger, the tale of Antar.

An epic tale.

Breeding

The nature that's in the body will only change in the winding shroud.

If his nurture did not improve him the stick will not correct him.

Two-thirds of the child is from its maternal uncle.[27]

This is part of the sales patter used by a matchmaker in introducing a girl as a suitable bride on the basis of the superior qualities of her family.

The bad one is my uncle; I am his sister's son.

If the mare's sire be noble then the more she is worked the more she'll improve.

This cub is from that lion.

True as a cheque/deed.

Self-proving and legal; also used sarcastically.

Khāndān

---

[27] There are variations, e.g. two-thirds of the righteous child are from his maternal uncle, two-thirds of the vices from the paternal uncle.

A youth of good character and honourable family.

Abū l-'Ayba (gold).

Pure 24-carat; also used sarcastically.

This cake is from that dough.

Kneaded in one's own blood.

Her light dazzles the seventh heaven
and blinds them that envy
In her own blood she is kneaded
her cheeks, O people, are wheaty

All you get from the ironmonger is sparks.

True to his profession/nature.

If it has a hole, it'll leak.

The vessel leaks what it contains.

The fire leaves only cinders.

Fāṭima, daughter of Faṭṭūma.

Like mother, like daughter.

A Kashān rug.

A superior type of rug attributed to the city of Kashān in Iran.

They placed the dog's tail 40 days in a bamboo cane – still it's not straight.

The same *ṭāṣ*[28] and the same *ḥammām.*

It is the same ass, only the horse-cloth has changed.

The moon is announced by its crescent.

A scorpion by nature.

The eloquent cock will be heard even while still in the shell.

His oil has seeped.

His true nature has been revealed.

A saline land is barren.

A slave is still a slave, even when he becomes the master.

The rose smells sweet even when faded.

If his father was onion and his mother garlic, how can he be sweet-smelling?

By his deeds you will know his lineage.

A ship on a flat roof.

Not behaving in accordance with its true nature.

---

[28] A metal dish used, inter alia, in the ḥammām to scoop water to pour on oneself.

Business

At Allāh's door.

Opening the door of his business, trusting that Allāh will provide.

Measles and smallpox.

Said of starting a new business: trouble all round.

The morsel has reached the mouth.

A successful outcome.

You are fully wholesome, O *kabar*.

An expression used in the market place as sales patter, whatever the merchandise on offer, to attract buyers. *Kabar* is a kind of thorn that grows in the wild and is supposed to have beneficial medicinal qualities.

I whistle me a tune and eat a date.

In the absence of customers.

Income and expense.

Alluding to complicated business affairs.

A sale and a clearance.

Utter failure.

Puncture.

Bankruptcy.

That was a black day when I met Cooper
they fined me and left me puncture[29]

Buy and sell, and your name will not perish.

The bazaar recognises neither father nor mother.

Knives are sharpened on door-steps.

The carpenter's door is always broken.

He who works, eats.

The white *qirsh*[30] will be useful in a black day.

To buy a winepress he sold the vineyard.

For every grape a thousand wasps.

Alluding to competition.

Sell rather than mortgage/pledge.

He who lends and borrows sinks without trace.

Better a pain in the eye than the worry of debt.

---

[29] The reference is to al-Karkhī's condemnation for libelling one Mr Cooper, resulting in a fine which was doubled on appeal.

[30] Ottoman small coin.

He who buys wine on credit becomes doubly drunk.

Opportunity passes as a cloud.

They told the haberdasher, your father is dead; he said, let me finish the deal first.

He who comes late will miss the dinner.

He who does not lose does not learn.

Of the cheap things that you buy, half are lost before you get home.

The capital is lost with the account.

A bad year has fourteen months.

A night bargain.

A bad deal made in ignorance of the facts.

There is no sharing in bargaining.

You have eyes to see and money in your pocket!

An exhortation to be vigilant and careful about what you buy.

If you do not buy from him or sell to him, not fall out with him, not lend to him or borrow from him, then you do not know him.

He who counts a lot loses a lot.

A Bedouin's count.

Inexact.

A Jew's count.

Precise.

Better an argument at the beginning than a dispute at the end.

An exhortation to agree all the details of a bargain at the outset.

If your market is hot, boil dogs and sell them.

In a strong market you can sell anything at all.

Receipts and expenses.

Plāgīm.

'Money', in colloquial Baghdadi Jewish dialect.

Like flies stuck to flypaper.

Industrious.

It is not every day that an ass dies in the ditch.

A saying to justify a price increase.

Anecdote: a man entered a restaurant one day and ordered a dish of kebab for which he was charged ten fils. He returned the following week and ordered the same dish. At the end of the meal he offered ten fils, but the restaurateur demanded 20. The customer remonstrated that he had been charged only ten the week before. The restaurateur responded as above.

God's business is the drops of the *ḥubb* (earthenware cooler).[31]

Your partner is your opponent.

The pot of the partnership does not boil.

You can find everything in the market except love.

When a merchant criticises the merchandise, it is because he wants to buy it.

Start selling shrouds, and they will stop dying.

Take the honour and leave me the profit.

Too much business, less profit.

Calamity

What is the colour of death? Reddish yellow?

The more it is shared the easier it feels.

Blindness in the dark.

If it is fated you will not know what hit you.

The axe has fallen on the head.

Enough to turn the hair of the suckling child grey.

We have torn the drum and given up singing.

---

[31] See note 25.

I am drowning – why should I fear the rain?

They put sackcloth on him.[32]

They were hit by a *'uwayna* ('little eye').

The evil eye; also, the little glass eye that is affixed to the street door to ward off the evil eye.

Neither *ān* nor *dān.*

Persian, *an* ('man'), *dan* ('place') – hence, utter desolation.

The hidden one is worse.

The respect has gone, lost with the capital.

He washed his hands.

The reference is to the end of the meal, or alternatively, to the washing of hands after a burial or a visit to the graveyard.

You were afflicted by one (a female), O Umm Hussain, but before you even became aware of it, the one became twain.

The allusion is to a husband acquiring another wife.

The hole is big while the patch is small.

Scraping the palm of one hand with the other.

[32] It is also prison garb.

To the blindness, smallpox is added.

Harder than death is killing yourself to avoid it.

Caution

When a great man becomes a bridge, take the long way round.

If you go to the king's reception enter the hall and leave it dumb.

Beware the smouldering coal under the ashes.

Trust in God but tie your camel.

Holding the rope by both ends.

Unguarded property teaches people to be thieves.

He who speaks the truth will lose his head.

He who speaks the truth will have a threadbare skull-cap.

> The implication is that it becomes threadbare with the slaps for punishment.

When you speak, do not fear, when you fear, do not speak.

> Do not force me to tell the truth, O deputy
> and reveal all that's in my heart
> For then I would be tearing the sheet and smashing the jug
> bleating *bā bā* in all directions
> Such as to cause the earth to split
> and the mountain to founder

When you kill a snake, be sure to smash its head.

Who can tell the lion it has bad breath?

Not every cloud sheds rain.

Kiss the hand you cannot bite, and pray for it to be broken.

> I fear to speak lest they hang me
>   or for life imprison me
> In sackcloth dress me
>   and set me to clean the privies

If your enemy is a fox, gird yourself as a lion.

A stalk with the grape.

> An exhortation to be wary of even a little stalk as one puts the grape in one's mouth.

Ask about the neighbours before the house.

Do not open a door unless you can close it.

A greeting leads to talking, and talking leads to the melons.

Do not cast a stone in the dark.

> Not knowing whom it might hit.

You see him as if he is walking on eggs.

You climb the ladder step by step.

If you knew what was in the sea you would not drink from it.

There is no security in three things: the sea, the Sultan and Time.

Clean your house, you do not know who may visit. Wash your son's face, you do not know who may kiss it.

Certainty

Hasan, brother of Hussain.

All read.

No need to enquire any further.

The earth will gather.

There is no escape from death.

The tongue may lie, but the money does not disappoint.

It does not require going to the qāḍī [judge].

From the time of the stick of Moses.

Settled a long time ago.

The river runs, and the folk know.

Hearing is not the same as seeing.

Do not start to say 'one' [i.e. begin to count] until they are in the saddlebag.

This year is it!

That is what cleric and soothsayer will tell you, and they will not be proved wrong, however it turns out.

One half of a thousand is five hundred.

Charlatanism

He lifts a slipper off the barefoot and hair off the bald.

He showed me the stars of midday.

The reader is Indian and those who beat their breast (in lamentation) are the *mu'dan.*[33]

Lamenting without understanding.

The orator is an Indian, the muezzin is of Shammar [hence Arabic-speaking] and the audience are Kurds.

That is a *qawāna* (gramophone record).[34]

Some tall story; a spin!

His word is equal to his piss.

He walks the earth and covers the sky.

He plays on the rope.

The allusion is to a circus gymnast on the high wire.

[33] See note 20.

[34] The word may be taken as derived from *qayna* (singer).

He can sell me a *kalak* [raft].

A *kalak* is a traditional river raft made of skins and assembled at the beginning of a journey. It is then loaded with goods and floated downriver. When it reaches its destination the goods are unloaded and the *kalak* broken up. Hence, to buy a *kalak* is to acquire something ephemeral or illusory.

He makes the gold to equal the copper.

That is not the talk of a quarter.

A quarter of a bottle of *'araq* (arak, an Iraqi alcoholic drink). The saying is based on the following anecdote: a man goes to a bar and consumes half a bottle, but when it comes to settling the account he disputes the bill claiming that all he had was a quarter. The barman says to him sarcastically: that is not the talk of a quarter!

It's meat from your bull.

Selling you what you already own.

He takes your money and mocks your chin.

He played on their brains as one plays with a ball.

What the thief leaves goes to the fortune-teller.

I would sooner steal from the mosque than from you, he says!

The talk of the night.

He takes you to the river and brings you back thirsty.

A tablet of soap in a pan of water.

He sells fish to the fish in the sea.

The soothsayer is a liar even when he tells the truth.

Lamenting those who spoke the truth.

> Based on a story: they told the wolf, we are going to let you loose among the sheep; he began to cry. They asked him why he was crying; he replied: I am mourning for those who spoke the truth.

Comeuppance

Him you cannot beat, leave to God.

God waits 40 years.

God is bigger than the Sultan.

O tyrant, you will have your day!

The beard of the greedy is up the arse of the penniless.

He who knocks on the door shall hear the reply.

He farted.

> Said of someone who sets out on some enterprise with great zeal only to return empty-handed.

He came back with a hernia.

He spits at the sky.

> The spittle will fall back on his head.

Licking his own spit.

She pondered her two men and did not get *Sayyid* ‘Alī.

> The reference is to a woman who alienated her husband in the hope of exchanging him for better, then ended up with neither.

He who is not content with a share (of a benefit) will end up having the whole shit.

The wrong that he does, God will visit it on him manifold.

The nine for ten, and shit right up to the throat.

> This is commonly understood to refer to a popular anecdote. A cleric in a mosque exhorted his listeners to give alms to the poor: whoever gives one to the poor shall be rewarded with two, he declared. A simple-minded listener thought he would do well by giving away ten liras to the poor. Having done that, he waited patiently for the reward until one dark evening, walking the street, he fell into a privy. Feeling a bag at the bottom he picked it up, took it home and discovered that it contained nine liras. On his next visit to the mosque he heard the same cleric declaim that whoever gave one to the poor would get it back doubled. Not so, called out the man: the nine for ten and ...

The morsel in his mouth turned out to be made of brick.

At the end of the day the drumbeat of the wedding feast will be heard.

> Indicating a disappointment; the origin may be an anecdote relating to an unsuccessful plot to thwart a wedding.

He steals the stick of the thief.

> The inference being that he would be bound to get his comeuppance.

He went in with two horns and came out with one.

If you laugh when you sell, you'll cry at the counting of the proceeds.

When the camel put on horns they cut off its ears.

His skin to the tanner.

> A shortened version of the saying: what the goat eats (gall-nuts) the tanner will get out (gall-nuts being used in tanning).

He thought it was meat, it turned out to be a lump of coal.

He killed the food, but did not eat it.

> He died before he could eat it.

Compatibility

Molasses and cream.

Warp and weft.

Two bottoms in one pair of underpants.

You scratch my back, and I scratch yours.

It is possible for a date to stick with another, but not for two straws.

The ten fitted together.

> The reference is to the fingers, hence a handshake.

Among the one-eyed close one eye, and close them both among the blind.

Fitting the *manqala.*

> *Manqala* is a Baghdadi game, normally played in the home. It consists of a board of two halves, each containing seven round holes known as *khānāt* (sing. *khān*). The object is to fill the holes of the player's half part with grains, seven to a hole.

Do not put the mangy next to the healthy.

Throw a man in the sea and he becomes a fish.

After living with people for 40 days, you become one of them.

Take the leaf from the lettuce, the soup from the meat, and the sweat from the *ḥammām.*

Wear the silk and befriend the Emir.

After bread, tobacco.

Contentment

I lick the strop and live contented.

> Based on an anecdote involving two mice, one living in a grocer's shop and boasting about his life of plenty while constantly in peril, the other living in a barber's shop and contenting himself with licking the strop used to sharpen the razor.

The low land drinks its own water and receives the waters of others.

Kiss your own hand and put it on your head.

> Alluding to the manner of expressing gratitude for a reward by kissing the hand of the donor, then lifting one's own hand to touch one's head.

Bread and onion and peace of the heart.

> Variants: Bread and onion are enough to fill the stomach.
> Barley, bread, and water from the well (Bedouin).

What you receive is what you were allotted.

Look down and not up.

As long as the sun shines there is a livelihood.

Our cattle are at home.

Coffee, tobacco and no worry.

If you miss the meal, say 'Bon appétit'.

Corruption

May God protect the grove from its watchman.

Baghdad is built with dates – demolish and eat *khastāwī.*

The *khastāwī* is a popular and superior variety of date.

The dates that you ate, their stones are in my pocket.

I know full well what you have been up to.

Go and laugh in your pocket.

Alludes to a corrupt payment hidden in a pocket, the 'pocket' referred to being that of a traditional Arab robe, i.e. in the space next to the chest, above the belt.

Oil the strap and it will glide.

Shīsh[35] and *kabāb.*

Illicit receipts.

[35] Skewer.

Neither *shīsh* nor *kabāb.*

Sea-green incorruptible.

He sold himself for the skin of an onion.

Strike with the five.

The reference is to one who, sitting with others to eat off a large circular tray, grabs the food greedily. This is traditionally done with the fingers (hence 'with the five') of the right hand, the left hand being considered unclean, since used in ablutions.

If fish eat fish, what will be left for the fishmonger to eat?

The sun has risen to expose the thieves.

The eye of the sun will not be blocked by a sieve.

The allusion is to the sun as an inspector watching the malefactors.

He is like a file!

The allusion is to the filing of coins.

A butchers' competition.

This refers to a false sheep auction with bidders in league with each other.

It is from the head that the fish first stinks.

If turbans float, so do rotten melons.

Crisis

You and your Lord, O Moses!

Cast me in the river, but give me a long life.

He moved away from the rain and found himself under a waterspout.

Come on, mule, help me carry it.

What crisis? A mere drink.

A crisis that ended in relief was no crisis.

A bottleneck from the door to the pulpit.

Pitch stuck to white linen.

A problem, and ever the rope shall be pulled.

> The allusion is to the labour of hauling a boat in a river against the stream.

Like a pigeon that's lost its dovecote.

More complex than a lizard's tail.

Hot is the iron.

Sitting on the sharp end of a pole.

A thousand sparrows will not fill the pot.

Criticism

Go, look in the mirror.

If the camel could see its ears it would be amazed.

The carcass does not corrupt the ocean.

The moon is not affected by the barking of dogs.

He who shows me his fault diminishes mine.

Criticising a stranger is folly; criticising a relative is concern.

For the camel to see its hump it would have its neck broken.

One who praises and criticises is a liar twice over.

There may be much truth in a lie.

They threw him into a blazing fire – he said the faggots were green.

The crow told the raven, you have a black face.

They told the camel: why are your legs bent? He replied, I see them straight.

Death covers all faults.

Cruelty

A sparrow in the hands of a child.

A *maḥmūdī.*

A slap attributed to an Ottoman officer of that name, so ferocious as to knock the victim down.

Make one shit lentils.

Giving one a hot wound.

An injury not felt immediately.

A heart of stone.

Sending one's skin to the tannery.

Sewing off one's mouth.

Cutting off one's tongue.

Showing one the midday stars.

Putting one's head in a hole.

Cynicism

The string is lost with the sparrow.

The reference is to one catching a sparrow and tying it in a string; the sparrow escapes with the string.

We gave up on the grapes – we only want our basket.

He went in tall and came out broad.

The wolves have become jackals.

Go and plant wool [or dung] and wait for the sheep to grow.

Drummers we have become in the time of the plague.

How many Solomons were undone by Solomon!

When the camel stumbles, that is when many knives come out.

He is digging a well with a needle.

The land does not betray its trust.

The allusion is to graves.

You'll hear the screams at the end of the night.

As the householders get up to find they have been burgled.

Go and entrust fat to the cat!

Better to follow the one who makes you cry than the one who makes you laugh.

Go to '*Ayn al-tamir*[36] to skin ants.

If every barking dog were given a brick to eat, each *mithqāl*[37] of mud would be worth a dīnār.

The thorn grows in the garden, the rose in the dung heap.

---

[36] The name of a place notorious for being malarial.

[37] A small weight; see note 16.

If you want rabbit, take rabbit; if you want deer, take rabbit.

> This is based on a story involving a lion and a fox who between them had caught a deer and a rabbit. Said the lion to the fox, if you want the rabbit you can have the rabbit; but if you want the deer then you can have the rabbit. Replied the fox, the deer is certainly your share of our enterprise, but I doubt whether it would be enough for you. I suggest you take the rabbit as well – one of its thighs is enough for me!

The faces are compatible, the hearts at odds.

The count is in the *ḥammām.*

Some are given walnuts [which are hard to shell], others are given figs.

Some sleep on the floor, others on the couch.

Whenever anyone dies, all you can say is: aye, God have mercy on him.

You do the account, and God will do the audit.

Decorum

Eat what pleases you, but wear what pleases others.

Eat, suit!

> A good apparel is a means to profit.

Immodest dress does not last; if it did, it would not warm.

Dress a swarthy man in red and laugh at him.

Dressed in rags and following the aristocrats.

Silk goes with everything.

You may meet the enemy hungry, but do not meet him naked.

The coffee is black, but it brightens the face.

We put on linen, and forget the hardship.

If you eat garlic, sit with the donkeys.

From your dinner to the lighting.

Economise on food, but make sure of good lighting.

Despair

The ultimate state.

It was missing a part, now it is complete.

Neither flying nor perched.

The allusion is to a bird, hence difficult to shoot or catch.

Broken is the hubble-bubble.

Dyeing the clothes of mourning.

Going the way of al-Ta'ma's cat.

One Hussain al-Ta'ma for ever mourned his cat, which had disappeared without trace.

The house is in ruins.

Like the owl of ruins.

The knife has reached the throat.

Our time is ended – the sparrow has eaten our dates.

It has become a 'Black Nine'.

> The allusion is to the Jewish lamentation on the anniversary of the destruction of the Temple on *tish'a bi-āb* (i.e. the ninth day of the Jewish month of Āb) in 586 BC.

Discord

I in one vale and you in another.

Two cannot play on the same rope.

Your fingers are not all of one length.

If the cat and the mouse made it up, the ship would be ruined.

Iron hitting iron

The world is upside down and the horses are stolen.

Every man carries a Satan in his pocket.

One hand in God's hand, the other in Satan's.

This is one thing and that is one thing.

One pulls by the long end, and the other by the short end.

A diet for the sick, pickles added!

The burden of an enemy is lighter that an argument with a friend.

The doors of Baghdad can be closed shut, not so the mouths of the troublemakers.

The heat is in the heart of the cucumber.

> This is based on the belief that the cucumber has a hot nature notwithstanding its cool appearance.

Two are brothers, three friends, four discord and mischief.

It is the Resurrection, the cauldron is boiling.

Dishonesty

Bent as a sickle.

Like the file.

> The allusion is to the use of a file to shave a coin.

I carried him behind me and he put his hand in the camel bag .

Your barley and not his wheat.

God knows whose dirhams they are.

> Anecdote: an illiterate Bedouin holds a ceremonial dinner in memory of his deceased father, in the course of which he pays

some dirhams to a *qārī* (reciter) to say a prayer for the deceased. Told after the ceremony that the *qārī* had duplicitly recited the prayer for another deceased instead, the Bedouin responded as above, to the effect that God will nevertheless acknowledge for whose benefit the money had been spent.

He shoes his horse the wrong way round.

To mislead his pursuers as to his direction of escape.

He who steals a minaret has to find a place for it.

A dishonest man may be betrayed by a single true word.

The poor do not lock their doors.

A well-composed lie is more credible than a wild truth.

He is accused of stealing rainwater from the waterspout!

He who steals a chicken will steal a camel.

Go and entrust the fat to the cat!

I do the lamentation, you do the rummaging.

This refers to a case of two dishonest confederates: one joining in the lamentation to distract attention, and leaving it to the other to find what there is of value to steal.

You keep quiet, I keep quiet, and we share the loot.

You do the accounts; God will be the auditor.

This would be said by a sleeping partner to the other partner, the manager of the undertaking.

The seeds are in your hands, and God is above you.

These words refer to a landowner as he supplies seeds to the farmer with whom he will be sharing the produce; they invoke the latter's conscience.

A *dallal* (broker; commission agent) of Sūq Haraj (a street market for second-hand goods).

Dishonour

Face covered in soot.

Generally connoting the loss of innocence and virtue.

His/her face was blackened by the soot from the bottom of the cooking pan.

A wedding with arms.

The allusion is to a wedding reception or demonstration at which there is a display of swords or swordplay. The reference in this context is to public disgrace.

He has become a spectacle.

O girls, is Ahmad one of you?

Accusing Ahmad of being effeminate.

Come out sun, and see them come out.

To the coward the whole world is not big enough.

Cover your heads, O bald ones!

Begging is an alchemy.

His mouth is closer to him than his mother's.

Disloyalty

A witness from my own household brought about my hanging.

He wears his face back to front.

Like the straw with water underneath it.

He dug a 'blind' well for me.

> A well with a deceptively concealed entrance.

You were silver and turned out to be coal.

I fed him a load of meat!

> The disloyalty towards the friend/acquaintance is implicit in the exclamation, since the speaker would not otherwise have talked of feeding him.

To the scorpion the boot.

When the camel stumbles the knives come out.

Disorder and unrest

A contract with the Angel of Death.

Halley's comet passed over them.

The Resurrection is come, the cauldron is boiling!

If you want to fill the well, demolish a minaret.

The wolves have become jackals.

The wolf is loose among the sheep.

Every man carries Satan in his breast pocket.

The sack is biting the mouse.

The rot starts in the head.

Strike the *khashm* (nose) and the eyes will well up.

Strike the leaders and their followers will take note.

He who is without a sheikh is led by Satan.

A *ṣūfī* proverb; the sheikh in the context is a *ṣūfī* leader.

The best of good manners is obedience.

He who moved it will hold it.

The head is no more, O 'Abbās.

The reference is to the head of the queue, hence no more orderly queuing.

They beat his back, he beats the one in front.

Every one/ten under a star.

They are all over the place; utter disorder.

Everyone to himself.

Qāl and *Qīl* (a hubbub).

Lawja.

A heated and disorderly argument.

A *ḥammām* of women.

A house of the deaf.

All talking and no one listening.

A sand-storm from the land of Babylon.

A sandstorm is a frequent occurrence in Baghdad, particularly after a spell of hot weather. It blows from the west, hence from the direction of Babylon.

The tear has got bigger.

A green faggot for the price of a dry one.

A faggot, in normal circumstances, commands a lower price before it is dried.

The *ḥubb* is broken!

ḥubb is a tall earthenware vessel. The saying can also be used to describe a falling-out between friends/lovers.

The weighmaster farted and the count was lost.

The suggestion is that his embarrassment caused him to lose count.

The cat's away – play mouse!

Better 100 years of tyranny than a night of anarchy.

Too much beating and the solder will yield.

I pull him towards the pulpit, he pulls me towards the tavern.

Doubt

To doubt is to be wise.

Our gunpowder is in Persia and your bullets are on the way.

You have to break the shell before you can eat the walnut.

Like the peacock, neither bird nor camel.

Like a winter's day.

It cannot be trusted.

But for the doubt in the air everyone would have gone to heaven.

This is one of the 40!

No one knows which pip has the blessing.

> The pomegranate is highly prized, and the saying alludes to the belief that one of the pips is from Paradise.

If two people tell you that your head is not on your shoulders, shake it.

Not even a *pāra* for your *qirsh.*

> Ottoman currency; 40 *pāra*s equalled one *qirsh.*

When a man hears his own lie at the far end of the market he begins to wonder if it is true.

A rumour does not spread for nothing.

The doubt of the hard of hearing.

The English/Abū Nājī

The sobriquet was first given to the English (meaning the British) after the First World War, then by extension to all English-speaking nationals. It is usually a mark of respect in Arab culture not to call people by their first name, unless they are intimates, but to address that person instead as the father/mother of his/her eldest son, or eldest daughter in default of a son.

Your God has brought it to you, O cock!
  it's that Abū Nājī loves you
Begone and laugh in your pocket
  you have become an eminent Deputy whose hand is in the fat.

Abū Najjāwī (diminutive of Abū Nājī).

Onions and fat is my soup
  and of the dates my share is the stones
My skin is stuck to my bone
  that's Abū Najjāwī's prescription for me

Abū l-Shafqa.

Beware the one with the *shafqa* (hat, derived from the French *chapeau*, through Baghdadi Jewish *shapqa*).

Al-Mister.

Englishman/ English speaker.

Krīmāwī.

Literally, one from the Krīmāt quarter of Baghdad, where the British Embassy is situated; part of the post-2003 invasion 'Green Zone'.

Abū Nājī is our Minister's uncle on his father's side.

This refers to the common saying that two-thirds of a child's bad character derive from the paternal uncle.

Some borrowed English words:

Bigrāj	Garage
Almis	'The Miss', referring specifically to Gertrude Bell, the Oriental Commissioner.
Nawṭ	Banknote
Rabl	A horse-drawn carriage. Originally a *landawn* (landau), it was later replaced by a carriage with 'rubber' wheels, hence *al-rabl.*
Alrayl	Specifically the 'Railway Company'.
Awfīs	Office
Awtail	Hotel
Bagad	Bucket
Buṭul	Bottle
Bidbul	At the double!
Charchal	Churchill
Coda	Quota
Darnaga	Drunk
Fanash	Finish

Fisglāṣ	First class
Galawsh	Galosh
Hulṭ	Halt
Iblawkī	Bloke
Jākī	Jockey
Jigāra	Cigarette
Kawb	Cup
Kirnilwāris	Cornwallis (at one time British Ambassador)
Kirnil	Colonel, and specifically referring to any one of the British Ministerial advisers.
Leftin wa-raytin	Left and right
Puncher	Puncture
Pāwnāt	Pounds
Piāda	Pedestrian
Pis-wal-awrāt	Please and alright
Prazanta	I presented myself to him.
Rajistrī	Registered (i.e. the genuine article)
Raysis	(Horse-)racing

Rost	Roast
Shawfar	Chauffeur
Sintirī	Sentry
Soljarī	(of) a soldier
Tampa	Stamp (for making impression or mark on a document)
Tanka	(water-)tank
Tāmsī	Englishman (from the Thames)
Tuck wa-finsh	Ticked and finished
Tiatru	Theatre
Wannak	You win
Warwar	Revolver

Exaggeration

Beating the drum and blowing the *mizmār* (an oboe-like instrument).

The river is soup, the trees spoons.

The best of the poetry is the lies.

A drummer's own wedding (and see below, **Self-reliance**).

A *dallāl* who lost his donkey.

> A *dallāl* is a selling or other agent. A person who had lost something would employ him to go round the town calling out the description of the lost object and the reward on offer for its return. The implication in the saying is that since it is the *dallāl*'s own donkey that is lost he would be making more and more noise.

Experience

He who is bitten by a snake will fear the pulling of a rope.

He who suffered a sting knows what's in the sac.

If this turns out to be like the other, what soup and what chicken!

Better the experienced than the wise.

The householder knows what is in his house.

I am its father and mother.

The contents of the pot are revealed by the spoon.

The experienced is better than the genius.

He who is one day older than you is a whole year wiser.

Give the dough to the baker woman to bake, even if she might eat half of it.

The son of the baker shall not die of hunger.

This is my own baking and my own cooking.

You will not appreciate my merits until you have tried others.

He whom you know is better than the stranger.

An apologia for nepotism.

Exploitation

On top of the load, some more.

The allusion is to a merchant employing a *ḥammāl* (porter) to convey a load in return for a fixed sum. After the goods are loaded on the back of the *ḥammāl*, and as he is about to go on his way almost doubled up by the weight, the merchant surreptitiously adds some more on top.

This bag on that *kalak*.

As in the preceding example, but with *kalak* instead of *ḥammāl* (a *kalak* is a flat-bottomed river craft for transporting goods).

The *ḥammāl* farts, the *sayyid* (the gentleman/master)blows a strawberry.

ḥabtarī.

One who benefits from the labours of others while doing nothing to earn it; a parasite.

He learns *ḥijāma* on the heads of orphans.

In the procedure of *ḥijāma* (a moderate form of blood-letting) scratches are made on the head or the torso.

He seeks a loaf from the skin of the weak.

When you share the food with the blind, eat justly.

He ate my dates and left me the stones.

He ate, and followed it with water.

Inference being that what was expropriated can no longer be retrieved, analogous to a meal said to be 'killed' when followed by a drink of water.

The barefoot exerts himself, the one in boots feasts.

The allusion is to a poor *ḥammāl* carrying a rich man on his back across and along flooded/muddy streets.

He made me a bridge to cross over.

A wolf in the midst of sheep.

The fox's/lion's coat.

That refers to a story involving a lion and a wolf. One day the wolf came by a discarded woollen coat, which he wore, it then being a cold winter. The lion passing by, admired the coat and asked the wolf: Where did you get that coat? Replied the wolf: I made it myself, and if it pleases Your Excellency, it is yours to wear in good health. The lion then tried to put it on but it was too small for him; so he asked the wolf to make him one that fitted. The wolf agreed to do so, but required the lion to provide him with a number of lambs so that he could use their skins in making the garment. The lion complied with this, and they agreed a date for the completion of the work. But when the time came the wolf apologised, saying that he still needed more lambs. A further delivery of lambs was made, and another date set for the delivery of the garment; but the outcome was the same as before. This was repeated time after time until the end of winter, when the wolf, fearing discovery of his chicanery, made good his escape.

One man has his beard on fire, the other comes along to warm his hands on it.

Extremism/excess

Either burning at both ends or remaining in darkness.

Either drum and pipe or hook and rope.

His head is hot.

The frying pan is on fire!

A sour piss.

There is a voice in his head.

He has a fixation.

Ten fights an hour.

> We know that you are fasting, but why get into a fight with everyone ten times an hour?

He fights his own *zīg*.

> The *zīq* (pronounced *zīg*) is the 'pocket' or top of the garment (above the belt), covering the torso and including the collar.

A mendicant with a dagger in his belt.

Either you let me play or I'll destroy the stadium.

He smashes the jar, and he's thirsty.

> Shut up! Don't let me smash the jar,
> I shall also smash the water melon and scatter the seed

He burns the blanket because of a flea.

He'd burn down a city to light a cigarette.

Too many blows and the solder will yield.

Too much and the cup will overflow.

Yatanamrad.

> He acts like Nimrod towards us (Nimrod is a legendary king famous for his cruelty).

He pinches Satan's bottom.

He carries his blood in the palm of his hand.

They told her to confine herself to the boudoir; she settled herself in the basket.

He gets himself drunk on a sultana.

Eye

The eye of the sun will not be blocked by a sieve.

His eye sees but his heart says: I'm sorry.

i.e. unmoved by what he sees.

His eye is strong.

He is rough, discourteous, unyielding.

His eye does not break.

He does not blink – he is obstinate.

'Uwayna.

Lit. 'little eye', referring to the evil eye warded off by the small eye of glass or similar material affixed to the outside of a dwelling.

They were hit by a *'uwayna.*

They suffered a setback brought about by the evil eye.

His eye is salt.

He is lustful.

His/her eye is not lowered

The person is disrespectful and/or shameless.

His eye is on the road.

Connoting a long wait.

Feud

There is Basūs war between them.

A pre-Islamic war between the tribes of Bakr and Taghlib that lasted 40 years, having started with a dispute over a she-camel by that name and the killing of one Klayb.

The blood of Klayb.

The Basūs war was started to avenge Klayb's blood.

Throw the stone back to where it came from.

It has got in the blood.

Blood has been shed, making it a blood feud.

A journey from which there is no return.

The soil does not drink blood.

The blood will not fade or disappear.

The bone is broken.

It is more than a dislocation.

The days are between us.

Getting set for a long dispute.

The rent is bigger now.

No alcove is left for a parley.

The traditional Baghdadi house consists of a central courtyard open to the sky with *īwāns* (partly enclosed alcoves or rooms) to the side. Hence the reference is to disputants trying to resolve their differences in some seclusion and privacy.

The cut caused by teeth will mend – not so the wound caused by the tongue.

The mother of the slain son sleeps; the mother of a son threatened remains sleepless.

If you feed them then let them be satiated; if you hit them, then let them feel the hurt.

The ultimate remedy is cauterisation.

This is based on the belief, particularly among the Bedouin, in the curative effect of fire or heat.

Chasing an opponent all the way to the graveyard.

The snake knows its killer.

The Bedouin took his revenge after 40 years, and said he had been quick about it.

Keeping a grudge longer than the camel.

God will not leave injustice unavenged.

God waits 40 years.

Let your eye be red but your grip gentle.

Blood that is not avenged will keep on questioning.

An old book, leave it closed!

The road for two quarrelling dogs leads to the butcher's.

The serpent will not forget its tail, the forester will not forget his son.

> This is based on a fable: A forester went out one day cutting down trees. As he was about to cut one, a serpent, whose home it was, asked him to spare it; in return it would pay him one gold sovereign every day. This arrangement continued for a while, until one day the forester was taken ill and sent his son to collect the coin. When the young man approached the tree, the serpent went into a hole and came back with the sovereign. The son, imagining that the serpent had a cache of treasure, lifted the axe and brought it down on the serpent, missing its head but severing its tail. In the same instant the serpent bit the young man, who died. Later, the forester approached the serpent wanting to renew the arrangement, in spite of what had happened. The serpent replied that this could not be: it could not forget its tail, just as the man could not forget his son.

Flattery

Sing a tune and hope for a date.

i.e., flatter and hope for a preferment.

He dances to whoever claps for him.

They cast grains before him.

The reference is to luring a pigeon.

Who dares tell the lion that its mouth smells?

The mule of the *Qāḍī*.

This refers to a popular anecdote. A *qāḍī* (cleric/magistrate) had a beautiful mule, of which he was very fond; he would take it every day to the mosque. One day the mule fell ill, and people flocked to the *qāḍī* enquiring after its health. When it died a whole throng of them accompanied its body from the *qāḍī*'s house to the cemetery; some returned to join him in mourning. But when the *qāḍī* died no one followed his hearse.

They honour the dog to flatter its owner.

The dog's tail gains it food, and its mouth gets it a beating.

If you need a favour from a dog, call it *ḥajjī*.

Praise the Bedouin and take his ʻ*abāya*.

Praising the unworthy is like saddling an ass in silk.

Fear not the man who smiles – fear the man who pats your back.

He who praises and criticises lies twice over.

If you praise the bride you should also praise the hairdresser and the bride's mother.

It is wrong to praise a man to his face.

A liar needs a good memory.

I serve you, I do not serve the aubergine.

> This is based on an anecdote. It is said that Sultan Aḥmad II wanted to test the sincerity of his vizier, who was reputed to be a flatterer. The Sultan said: Yesterday evening I had a meal of aubergine which upset me. Commented the vizier: that's right – everyone knows that aubergine is heavy on the stomach. The following week the Sultan was heard to say that he had had a meal of aubergine which was the best he had ever eaten. Responded the vizier: there is no doubt that the aubergine is good for one's health. The Sultan then reminded the vizier what he had said just a week before, and asked him to explain. The vizier replied: I serve the Sultan not the aubergine!

He ignored father and mother, and praised his father's new wife.

Fortune

When it comes, the pigeon will be able to lay an egg on the wire; when it goes, the donkey will dare to piss on the lion.

Good fortune

The moon, the spring and being alive.

As long as there is coffee and tobacco.

The bird of good omen settled on his head.

Spring moon.

> The reference is to spending a moonlit evening in an orchard.

A 14th-day moon.

> i.e. the full moon, half way through its monthly circuit.

Golden luck.

Head of the water.

> The reference is to the first farmer in the queue to receive water from an irrigation canal.

His hand is in the fat.

His wealth is *tick* (unique).

The box of the *wilāyāt* (treasure-house).

Heaps of money, and the date trees are heaving.

Three things dispel the gloom: water, greenery and a pretty face.

Three things prolong life: a big house, a swift horse and an obedient wife.

A white banner.

> A banner of celebration as usually used in a parade of a boy or boys after circumcision.

They put gallnuts on him.

> Gallnuts are suupposed to have a magical protective quality; they are commonly put on a child to ward off the evil eye.

His bread is under the plate.

The lady sits on the bench.

Like the chicken – its livelihood under its feet.

More coming than going.

The bread is baked and the water is in the cup.

We sought it in the sky and found it on earth.

> Found it to be easier than we had thought.

Like the newborn lamb; if it looks down it's grass, if it looks up, milk.

Misfortune

He threw *gala* (blank, ineffective).

> The allusion is to the game of backgammon. The *gala* is a throw of the dice that fails to get the thrower out of a block.

He escaped the wolf and was eaten by the lion.

He fell in the *manganelle.*

> A military engine used in sieges.

He is left sitting on the mat of poverty.

> Like a mendicant.

Nothing will be seen of them, not even the smoke of the fire.

Wash your hands of them.

> Said to signify that they are utterly lost; the allusion being to funeral rites.

I was silver, and became coal.

Mupunchir.

> Bankrupt, a corruption of the English 'puncture'.

In the end I lost the string as well as the sparrow.

I wiped my hand on the wall.

Said to describe utter desolation.

His pocket is pressed with a hot iron.

i.e. empty.

His head is stuck in a hole.

My money is the currency of lentils and onions.

The food of the poor that fills the stomach without giving much nourishment.

A harvester whose sickle is broken.

Our ewer/jug was broken.

There is a Baghdadi superstition that breaking a receptacle in one's household on the first day of the year presages bad luck.

The horse and not the horseman.

Rather lose the one than the other.

The cauldron (masc. gender) has become a pot (fem.).

Thus doubly reduced.

He has a hernia.

Our home was in Qanbar 'Alī – how is it we are now in al-Jawba?

Qanbar 'Alī is a poor district of Baghdad; al-Jawba is still more inferior, being where the tanneries are situated.

From the minaret to the privy.

We have not done a good deed, so why the bad luck?

The allusion being to the perversity of the times punishing one for one's good deeds.

Black banner.

Friendship

Let the bitter be at the bottom and the sweet on top.

Stuck together with solder.

You can't clap with one hand.

The companion before the road.

A paradise without people is not worth living in.

The lads of the *garriya.*

Garriya is a corruption of *qarya* (village).

A Christian marriage.

A friendship for life.

Grass roots.

> The allusion is to networking, firmness and growth.

Guard your friend even in the fire.

A *dallāl* of people.

> A *dallāl* is a commission agent or broker employed for buying and selling. The *dallāl* of people is a good networker.

Two dates will stick each to each – but two dry peelings will not.

The passageway is narrow and dark; but every friend knows his friend.

A friend looks you in the face; an enemy looks down at your feet.

No one will befriend the owl except the crow.

The friend's flower hurts.

> The allusion is to a story: a criminal is suffering the ordeal of execution by stoning. He puts up stoically with every stone that is thrown at him but cries in anguish when a friend of his comes past and casts a flower at him.

His friendship is on his lap.

> A transitory friendship, like an object on one's lap which will fall when one gets up.

Stop your lamentation, O nightingale – passion will not last, nor friendship endure.

He who is with you, is with you; he who is against you is against you.

There is no embarrassment among friends.

He who does not guard the old will not enjoy the new.

He drank their water and became like them.

He who befriends the blacksmith will burn his clothes.

Sharing is a blessing.

There is no blessing in sharing.

Shortening by sharing.

> The allusion is to the shortened 'travellers' prayers' when travelling in a group.

The friend is bought and not sold.

Time fastens friendship, love unravels it.

The summer has parted from winter.

> A falling-out.

Beware your enemy once, but beware your friend twice.

Criticism between friends is soap for the heart.

> Clears the air and averts a falling-out.

A man's wealth is in his friends.

One candle can light another.

Buying and selling are measured in hundredweights, friendship in mithqāls.[39]

The heart is a canal.

The friend says, 'I told you so'; the enemy says, 'I must tell you'.

If you find your friend sweet, do not gobble him up entirely.

If you want to keep your friend, settle accounts with him every day.

> Variant: if you want to keep your friend, neither give nor take.

Eat the bitter, drink the bitter, but do not befriend the bitter.

Moses repudiated him, and Muhammad did not recognise him.

> A serious falling-out.

Futility

Will you ask who dug up the river, and who begat the bastard?

Ink on paper.

Cooking pebbles.

---

[39] A *mithqāl* is a small weight, see note 16.

A piss in the river.

Whether *ḥalāl* (meat of animal slaughtered ritually, hence clean) or not, it is already in our stomachs.

Wind in a net.

Like a toothless old woman desiring the seeds of a pomegranate.

> This might be connected with the belief that one of the seeds is from paradise.

How many pips in a pomegranate?

> i.e. more than one would bother to count.

The fart of a goat.

A fart in *sūq al-ṣafāfīr*.

> This is the copper market in Baghdad, where at any one time hundreds of coppersmiths work the metal sheets creating an enormous and continuous din.

A cobbler to the barefoot.

Going to Shfātha for a cure.

> Shfātha is a location notorious for being malarial.

All vain, the questions and the answers.

I put down everything on paper (i.e. calculated everything) except the skid!

Going to claim one's money from Dabash.

The reference is to a big scandal in which a financier, Dabash, went bankrupt, with the loss of his depositors' moneys.

Don't go chasing the wind that carried your hat away.

Striking a cold iron.

What good can the mouse find at the blacksmith's?

It was a bird, and it flew.

Garrulity

A *dallāl* who lost his donkey.

He had swallowed the tongue of the bird.

Not every tongue is a bulbul.

He is like a bee in a jar.

His tongue is long.

A scandal-monger, tell-tale.

Your tongue is your steed – guard it and it will guard you.

Muzzle your tongue.

Buy and do not sell.

i.e. listen in silence.

Listen with two and talk with one.

Two ears, one tongue.

The conversation stops when the food is served.

The longest prison sentence should be reserved for the tongue.

In the past, whoever spoke 100 sentences died.

An ‘*addāda* lost a relative.

The *‘addāda* is a professional mourner, whose principal task is to enumerate the virtues of the departed.

Variant: the ‘*addāda* laments her son.

One does not speak all one knows.

The key to eating is a morsel, the key to mischief a word.

Like bringing you a meatball from every pot.

The ear is not made to grow by what it hears.

From Damascus to Aleppo.

i.e. idle chatter all the way. A laconic opposite to this is: they asked him to tell the story of Joseph; he said, Joseph was lost and his father found him.

Generosity

Generosity covers all faults.

To him who presents you a mosquito, make him a gift of a camel.

Do good, and cast it in the river.

> i.e. forget it, and do not expect a favour in return.

Oil seeps from his elbows.

Barmakīs.

> The allusion is to the family of the Barmakīs, who were prominent courtiers during the reign of Harūn al-Rashīd and were celebrated for their liberality.

More liberal than the clouds.

Generosity is commensurate with what's available.

My house is mean, not I.

To be clean is to be pious.

> Cleanliness in this context is to be stripped of one's wealth through good deeds.

Food to the hungry and water to the thirsty.

An Emir making a gift of what is not his to give.

A favour cuts off the tongue.

Bread in the stomach of the noble is a debt, in the stomach of the vile, a charity.

A gift of an onion – all I remember of it is the bite and the tears.

If the Bedouin comes visiting, change your door.

> He would expect you to show him the generosity of the desert people.

When returning from a trip, bring back a gift even if it's a brick.

The river gives the dog and the lion to drink.

He calls *wayr.*

> This refers to a Baghdadi custom whereby the friend or acquaintance who is first to arrive at a teahouse will call *wayr* to the teahouse owner, as the other goes to pay for his drink – the caller is telling the owner not to accept payment from the other but to add it to his own account. That is analogous to, the situation of a host being hospitable in his own *muḍīf.* The custom has been known to apply even to one sitting in a bus, calling *wayr* at the arrival of a friend or close acquaintance. As one can imagine, the custom or practice can cause embarrassment.

Greed

He wolfed the food and the plate.

The hen dies with its eye on the dung heap.

When it comes to stomachs the eyes are blind.

Connotes the monopolising of good things.

He ate the heifer as well as the cow.

Pull out the tooth of greed!

Wipe your mouth!

You've had enough; the reference is to wiping the mouth at the end of the meal.

Your dīnārs are your religion.

His beard is up the arse of the bankrupt.

As soon as they are told to save water everyone starts to drink.

A man's eye is only filled by the earth.

He goes to the mosque and says he has a brother.

He is not satisfied by what he has been given to eat, and asks for more to take away, claiming it is for a brother.

A full stomach and a hungry eye.

Like the locust, eating more than its weight.

A free colocynth[40] is sweeter than sugar.

He eats with his hand as well as the ladle.

---

[40] a cucurbitaceous climbing plant of the Mediterranean and Asia, having bitter-tasting fruit (Collins English Dictionary, 30th Edition).

He chooses the figs to pick, even when they are unripe.

The stomach is full but the eyes are hungry.

Not even fire consumes all the logs.

Place the tray before him and all you will hear then is the ringing of the stones.

i.e. the stones from the fruit he is eating.

They gave him the Treasury – he asked: Where is the broom?

When the brains were divided, everyone was content with his brain; but when they allotted wealth, no one was happy with his lot.

Hardship

Zaqnabūt.

An indigestible meal.

Like the ant, carrying more than its weight.

A 14-month year.

The days of a month without bread are incalculable.

Better 1000 nights in the grave than one night in poverty.

What is there in the mosque for the thief to steal?

What story can the heart of the suckling child relate?

The *khān* (boarding house) has room for everyone except me and my donkey.

This appears to be a Biblical reference.

A patch on the shoulder.

Implying a repair to a worn-out jacket or robe.

Neither money for the Sultan to seize, nor a brain for Satan to remove.

He who does not fall does not rise.

Chewing one's own cud.

The price of chickpeas and onions.

The little one can afford.

Once the water is spilt it can no longer be collected.

Having no credit with anyone.

And ever shall the rope be pulled.

The allusion is to the hard effort of hauling a river craft upstream.

Neither a date in the hand nor one in the mouth.

More than an elephant can drink.

Seeing the stars at midday.

He who needs fire will hold it in his hand.

He who needs warmth does not resent the smoke.

Health

The best treatment is cauterisation.

> The Bedouin used it to strengthen arms and legs as well as for treating any illness, believing in the curative effect of fire. It is still practised in the rural areas of Iraq.

Cut your hand and pass among the crowd.

> In this way everyone will advise you on a remedy.

The physician's real skill is in relieving you of your money.

Before you reach a new town eat onions.

> Thought to protect against germs.

A day's fever will be followed by a year of good health.

May God grant health so long as the chickens are barefoot.

> Addressing a person by way of congratulating him on recovery from illness. In a similar vein: Ç̣elebrate, O beast, your hunter is dead!

The stomach is the home of illness, fever is the beginning of the cure.

May his belly be a drum and his legs ropes.

A change of air is better than any physician.

The pillow loves sleep.

> This is said to a sick, bedridden person to comfort him, taking his mind off the illness by attributing his confinement to love of sleep.

Health is measured in *mithqāls,*[40] illness in tons.

Heart

His heart is white.

> He is well-intentioned.

His heart is clear.

> He bears no grudge.

His heart is black.

> He is ill-intentioned.

His heart is chafed.

> He is sour/unhappy.

---

[41] See note 16.

His heart is trees.

He is amiable.

His heart is stone.

He is cruel/unyielding.

His heart is a sheet of paper.

He blows hither and thither – inconstant.

Hospitality

A guest brings the blessing with him.

Hospitality is for three days – after that put him to work, or show him the door.

The first day is a lantern, the second a handkerchief, the third a pig and son of a pig.

Guests and fish stink after three days.

When you want to get rid of a guest, start to sweep and dust.

The sun has come out, the sky is clear – there are no more excuses.

i.e. for the guest to remain.

The stranger is blind even though he is sighted.

He needs to be guided.

The stranger has no lover.

To visit and not to eat and drink is like visiting a graveyard.

All the stranger has is a *khān* (boarding-house) or the *ḥammām*.

Said to invoke hospitality.

Humiliation

He pulled a rag over his head.

Cast off the garb of shame and cover yourself with a mat.

If you are missing a hand cover the stump with your sleeve.

His nose is broken (see ***Khashm*** further down, and the reference under **Baseness** above).

Better to be in the first row of hell than live in the midst of slippers (i.e. women).

He presented himself and had his face slapped.

We offered all we had, but the buyers turned away.

You say what you like, and we will both eat.

A hungry mother urging her daughter to beg.

They knit a rope with his moustache.

You cannot muffle the beat of the drum by covering it with a carpet.

His face is blackened.

He was forced to swallow a pole.

Riding a donkey, back to front, with the tail in your hand.

They painted our banners black.

When your son grows a beard, shave yours off.

At the last reckoning our wool turned out to be red!

The cauldron (*qazān* masc.) reduced to pot (*qidr* fem.).

Lifting the skirt to cover the face.

Hypocrisy

Your *qirsh* is not even a *pāra.*

Ottoman currency: one *qirsh* equalled 40 *paras*.

Playing on two ropes at the same time.

Let your hand do the talking.

Pay what's due, instead of making excuses – your deed rather than your word.

He wears his face back to front.

Would you believe a donkey rather than me?

Anecdote: a man came knocking on his friend's door, asking if he could borrow his donkey. The owner, not wanting to comply, said that it was not at home – he had lent it to another man. At that moment the donkey, inside the house, was heard to bray. 'But isn't that your donkey I hear?' asked the visitor. The owner replied: 'Who would you believe, the donkey or me'?

A mirror at the front and a thorn at the back.

Bright faces and black hearts at morning prayers.

He who tells tales to you will tell tales against you.

His word and his piss are the same – 25-carat gold!

An Iblīs (Lucifer) in each fold of his turban.

Summer and winter on the same roof.

This alludes to the Baghdadi practice of spending summer nights on the flat roofs of their houses, and to the following anecdote. A woman gets up in the night and finds her son lying next to his wife. She advises her daughter-in-law to keep herself at a distance from him as it is too hot. The woman takes a few more steps, and comes by her daughter lying next to her husband. She tells her daughter to get closer to her man as it is cold. Hence the saying.

We saw you above and we saw you below.

Anecdote: a mendicant came to a house looking for alms. He knocked on the door and the housewife called out:

'I'm on the upper floor; if I had been below I'd have given you something.' The next time, the mendicant knocked and the housewife called out: If I'd been above I'd have thrown you something. The mendicant then said: 'O lady, we saw you above and we saw you below!

A pomegranate, but the heart is full.

Like the six-faced dice.

He advises the householder to be on his guard, and tells the burglar to steal.

Wait until your cart is overturned, then people will show you the way!

When the rich man eats a snake they say it is a good idea; when the poor man eats a snake they say he must be poor.

Impassivity – avoiding trouble

An eye that sees not and a heart that grieves not.

The eye sees and the heart says sorry.

He sees the suffering of others but only expresses regret.

Neither my camel nor my she-camel.

Not joining the caravan.

Home and bolt the door.

From house to mosque, from mosque to house.

If you fall out with your neighbour replace your door.

He who tries to reconcile two adversaries receives double the blows.

Neither a live coal in my hand nor a date in my mouth.

Deaf and dumb at the celebration.

The cat from the coal house.

Ṣāmūṭ, lāmūṭ.

> A distorted pronunciation (for emphasis) of *ṣāmit* (listener) and *lā māt* (he did not die) – hence, keeping quiet and surviving.

His head and the wall.

At the rising of the sun and at its setting, *khawājah*[42] 'Alī is *mullā* 'Alī.

> Continuing to be uninvolved.

Until you have reached the other side, go on calling the bear *'ammu.*[43]

---

[42] Mr.

[43] Lit. 'uncle', a respectful form of address, similar to 'sir'.

Indolence

Not stirring for a date.

One so lazy he lies under a date palm waiting for a ripe date to fall into his mouth.

A *mithqāl*[44] of laziness, a hundredweight of poverty.

Allāh will not bring it down to you in a basket.

The dogs of Qanbar 'Alī, replete in the shade.

Better a roaming fox than a sleepy lion.

He got up in the morning *darnaka*.

Darnaka (idle) is a corruption of the English 'drunk'.

He measures the shade and the sun.

He spends his day lounging in the shade and feels the progress of the sun.

He sleeps and his legs are in the sun.

In his long slumber he is unaware that his legs have become exposed to the sun.

He spends his day squashing nits.

The dog of the bazaar.

Hanging around doing nothing.

[44] See note 16.

The owl of the ruins.

He might as well castrate dogs.

The point of the saying is that dogs are neither castrated nor eaten.

You will not play if you do not bestir yourself.

The youth, the middle aged, the woman, the old man
they all came into this life to labour
The proverb tells us, and tells us true,
he plays, our readers, whoever exerts himself

Ingratitude

Beware the man whom you have done a good turn.

No load is heavier than gratitude.

The seal and the stamp are in my pocket.

It is to me that you owe the preferment.

Do not cast a stone in the well from which you drink.

A dog of two families.

Like the dog of Bahbahān[45] that bites the householder as well as the caller.

He pokes the eye of the sailor while riding in his boat.

---

[45] A town in Iran.

It is my fault I was bitten by the scorpion, since it was I who picked it up.

The favour that I did him was lost like a piss in the river.

He ate the dates and shat me stones.

He had fingers in the pot, and fingers in my eyes.

Do no good and you will not have heartache.

Having got herself a man, she complains that he is one-eyed.

Even the chicken is better, lifting its head to the sky as it drinks.

The living does not water the living.

Irony

The camel will only know its God when the going gets slippery.

No camel knows its God until it dies.

The camel that carries a prodigious load can be brought to its knees by adding a sieve.

If I do not eat it the lion will.

It is not the fire that makes the sweetmeat sweet.

Like a joss stick, you only get the incense when it burns.

God gives a walnut to the toothless.

He wants the shirt from off the man's back, and the man is naked.

The moon goes into eclipse when it is the orphan girl's wedding night.

The strong burglar asks the householder to help him carry the loot!

But for breakages the potter would go out of business.

If you do not want to give your daughter away, ask for more bride money.

What if the blind man stumbled and needed help? You are not more merciful than God.

He who is on his deathbed will settle for a fever.

He who is penniless is not worth a penny.

My only lovers are a dog and a heartless fool.

Said by a woman.

Do not fear God, fear him who does not fear God.

He can swallow a camel but choke on a mosquito.

We have despaired of the dates – all we want is our basket.

If it escaped the wolf, the lion will get it.

He avoided the rain and fell in the drain.

The men of Shammar are doing fine; all they want is food and linen.

> Anecdote: Farḥān Pasha, sheikh of the Shammar tribe, is sitting in his *dīwān* (public assembly room) when a man of his tribe arrives. The sheikh asks him how things are with him and his people. The man who had come to ask for help gives this sarcastic reply to indicate how hard up they are.

He who is drowning does not fear the rain.

See how the carcass floats in the sea while the pearl sinks.

The content of the pot is revealed by the spoon.

It is with poison that one rids oneself of poison.

> A reference to taking medicine (poison) as a cure.

The seal is my seal but blow me if I know what it (the document) means.

He dug up and buried.

> i.e. gilded the lily – often used to describe an erudite speech or presentation. The allusion is to funeral rites, from preparatory work up to their completion.

A cobbler for ‘Afaj.

> ‘Afaj was notorious for the fact that its inhabitants went about barefoot.

He came to add kohl and blinded her.

I brought the bald one to entertain me – he uncovered his pate and scared me.

If you wish to squander your wealth, buy an old house and restore it.

The drunkard does not count the cups.

We were not content with blindness – so we ended up with blindness and smallpox.

He who cannot dance blames the earth for not being straight.

Eggs will not be cooked by a fart.

It is only when your cart overturns that people will rush to show you the way.

My sister is dead; her dress fits me perfectly.

For excess of love the river swallows its progeny.

The judgment of Moses.

> The story goes that two quarrelsome men came before Moses to settle their bitter differences concerning the disputed ownership of a camel. 'Do you want my judgment or that of God?' asked Moses. 'God's', they replied. Moses then cut off the head of the camel and gave it to one of them, and left the rest for the other.

The judgment of Qaraqawsh.

> A fourteenth-century Emir, notorious for his erratic, cruel

and oppressive judgments, which became proverbial.

God's anger.

This expression (Baghdadi Jewish) is used to describe something as unbelievably wonderful; probably having its origin in the Biblical reference to the plagues of Egypt.

Blow – heaven is not Khān Jghān.

Khān Jghān is a busy market of goldsmiths and jewellers who at one time were mostly Jewish. The humorous story starts with an apprentice at the bellows questioning his employer: 'Master, do Jews go to heaven?' 'You idiot,' replies the master, 'heaven is made specially for the Jews.' 'What about Christians?' 'They are kept in the outer yard.' 'And the Muslims?' 'Go on blowing,' retorted the master, 'heaven is not Khān Jghān!'

Justice/Injustice

Rights require throats.

i.e. advocates.

We needed someone to help us, so we came to him – and found he was a Pharoah.

i.e. a despot.

For every judge in heaven there are at least two in hell.

A bribe removes the turban from the judge.

Sit crooked but judge straight.

> Better be just than correct in your interpretation of the law.

When the judge is against you, avoid his court.

Please God, give our judge much wisdom.

The court is not the judge's property.

Judge him for what he shows, not for what he hides.

> A man should not be punished for his inner thoughts.

The hand that is severed is free of blame.

> The punishment is full payment for the crime.

Two you do not upset: the judge and the physician.

> Variant: pray for absolution for your judge and your physician.

The law is to the sword (i.e, to the strong); it is the weak who needs witnesses.

Cursing is the weapon of the weak; strength is the sister of God.

Borrowed testimony.

> Bearing false witness.

You do the stealing and I'll testify.

Used sarcastically, and with a variant: a thousand witnesses for a dry peeling.

There is no offence in a thief stealing from a thief.

The thief is one, the suspects a thousand.

Said of the injustice of holding many people suspect when the offence could only have been committed by one person.

Beat all the passers-by until the guilty one confesses.

Confession is half the pardon.

He who does not accept the law of Moses will have to submit to the tyranny of Pharaoh.

He who sees injustice and keeps quiet is a dumb Satan.

To justice denied they added a beating.

To the drowning, a ducking.

Be cruel in equal measure and you will be just.

The fever enters from both feet.

It was a common superstition that illness entered the body through bare feet.

You are before the Lord, O Moses.

To him merciful and forgiving, to me a severe punishment.

When God wants to strike, He needs neither a stick nor witnesses.

The favour of the judge is worth two witnesses.

Justice is a sharp sword.

Our judge is a green scarecrow.

Better the tyranny of the cat than the justice of the mouse.

Neither claimant nor defendant.

> Anecdote: the court of a certain judge, Sheikh Ḥamīd al-Qāḍī, was boycotted because of his erratic judgments. He then set up a stall in the market place and had men arrested at random and brought before him to be examined, in the following manner: he started by asking the man if he had a claim against anybody – the man said that he had none. The judge next asked him if anyone had a claim against him – the man said that he knew of none. The judge called to his clerk to note down: neither claimant, nor defendant. Charge, one *majīdī.*

Beware the sea-green incorruptibles.

The bald-headed woman is made equal to the one with hair.

It is (only) the skin of the poor that is sent to the tannery.

If you eat with the blind, curb your appetite.

Drowning and condemned for making waves.

Let our judge be a saw, giving and taking.

> i.e. let him be impartial, sawing the wood with equal forward and backward cuts.

But who will read, who will listen?

> i.e. justice ignored and denied.

If you do not have the deeds in your hand, go and claim the money from Dabash.

> Dabash was a notorious financier who went bankrupt, losing a lot of people their money.

You might as well moisten the deeds and drink their water.

> This alludes to a common trick of a charlatan or witch doctor prescribing a magical cure, the process of which consists of the following: the illiterate client is given a piece of paper on which some words or diagram are written or traced, told to put it in a cup, pour water over it, and drink it while making a wish.

The lion is accused even though he went to sleep hungry.

Some eat the roast and others feel the smoke (from the spit) in their faces.

They condemned me for the evils that others did.

The lamb devoured the shepherd's bread.

> The allusion is to the lamb that is punished for devouring

the shepherd's bread – hence, a just sentence.

When you start a law suit you plant a date tree for your lawyer.

A retired judge cannot keep his mouth shut.

Peace is the last judge.

I do not fear the judge's punishment – it is God's mercy that I fear.

After 40 years, or 40 months, or 40 days.

God's retribution, and the mystical number 40.

Khashm

'Nose' in Iraqi dialect. While the moustache is associated with honour (swearing by one's moustache), the *khashm* is associated with manliness and pride.

He raises his *khashm* as high as the sky (in pride/haughtiness).

We know you are fasting
but why start ten fights an hour?
Your *khashm* is raised high in the air
as if you had lent ten million
Of the yellow ringing ones
to your Lord

A big *khashm*.

Arrogance.

His *khashm* is broken.

He has been humiliated.[46]

Dannich khashmak.

Lower your *khashm* – some modesty, please!

Yatkhashmir.

He is being disdainful.

Kinship

I and my brothers against our cousin; I and my cousin against the stranger.

I pray the prison for my brother (i.e. that he may be condemned to imprisonment) but hate whoever says 'Amen'.

If you want to know if a man is insane, curse his family and wait for the answer.

The father is a little God.

There is no time for charity when relatives are hungry.

For want of a provider we called the dog 'uncle'.

My heart is on the heart of my son, the heart of my son is on the stone.

---

[46] May be said to go back in time to the wars with the Byzantines, when prisoners often had their noses cut off.

It is the aunt and the cousin that I look after – to the stranger the leftovers.

You do not get with child by visiting shrines or by morning prayers.

It is better to have a mad son than a lady for a daughter.

One cannot return a gift to God.

The gift of a newborn daughter.

For want of a boy, we called the dog Yāsīn.

The last of my womb, daughter of my white hair, there is no shame in spoiling her.

The string of worry beads is complete.

A complete family; children of both sexes.

The son of your son is your son; not so the son of your daughter.

Nothing is dearer than a son except the son of a son.

The first son keeps your name alive.

The bone does not deny the flesh, nor the flesh the skin.

Satan does not destroy his own house.

Your family may cheat you, but they will not swallow you.

Boys of the quarter, every one knows his brother.

The bald woman boasts about her sister's hair.

Every bird to his own.

He lays himself down to sleep wherever the sun sets.

Said of the homeless wanderer, repudiated by his tribe.

If fish eat fish, what will be left for the fisherman?

If relatives fall out with each other, the result is utter failure.

When the angel of death appears, who does not direct him to his cousins?

Relatives are scorpions.

You no longer care for your beard once you are parted from it.

Yashwaynlī, yashwaynlī, your fire than my people's paradise

Yashwaynlī is an exclamation meaning 'Woe to me'. The saying is a bitter complaint about one's own kith and kin.

Beget bricks and bolster the house.

Referring to children.

From roses, thorns; from thorns, roses.

i.e. generational change.

My brother is his wife's brother.

A parade with swords.

> Generally alludes to circumcision, when boys who had been circumcised were paraded on horse-back, holding swords and preceded by drums and banners.

Marriage

He who does not sow in his youth will see his land arid and waterless.

When you feel depressed, marry.

He who marries his cousin will not be sorry.

If the cousin is available, the stranger is but an onion.

He who marries a stranger will not die from illness.

Do not marry a girl from a poor family – she will bring her poverty with her.

Marry off your daughter and free your house from shame.

Better a man with a trade than the man in a mansion.

One year to you, and one year to your child.

> A mother's advice to the bride.

One thousand men in the market, and no writing in my trousseau.

> 'Writing' refers to a marriage certificate.

Patience, daughter, and you will be lucky: either a woman dies or a stranger passes by or a lad grows to manhood.

The money of the avaricious is blessed when used as women's dowries.

Give the lad to the girl, and let them go their own way.

> This is heard from the father of the groom. The implication is that, contrary to common practice, he, as head of the family, would neither want them to live in his house, nor to have to maintain them.

Better a bachelor for an age than a widower for a month.

When a Bedouin comes by some money he spends it – either by buying a rifle, or buying a gun, or getting himself a wife.

Play with the figs until they mature.

> Advice to the groom of a pre-pubescent bride; the allusion is to her breasts.

I cared and I suffered, and now he is yours effortlessly.

> A conventional saying at a marriage celebration, the groom's mother addressing, and seemingly congratulating, the bride's mother.

Meddling

Curiosity does not sit well with a messenger.

Lamenting at every funeral.

Must have a part in every tale.

He has a relative in every slum.

She goes in with the groom and comes out with the bride.

An allusion to the wedding night.

The groom took the bride, and everyone else went home.

Stay in your land and guard your honour.

I counsel you, O heart, be neither guest nor host.

To every two he is a third.

He hastens to every drum beat.

It is the owner who is the seller, not the broker.

The salt of the kitchen – it must have a part in every dish!

He who knocks on the doors of others will hear the knock on his door.

He is neither Aḥmad nor Maḥmūd.

He who advises you to divorce will not provide the alimony.

She is ready to give evidence, even though she had not been there.

The judge is satisfied – what is it to do with you?

Moderation

The driblets of the *ḥubb.*

(For *ḥubb*, see **Disorder/Unrest**).

Stretch your legs only as far as the blanket will cover them.

Bread, onion and the stomach is full.

The diet is half the medicine.

Better short-sighted than blind.

It's the tall trees that are blown down by the wind.

Too much beating and the solder will give.

Too soft and you will be squeezed; too hard and you will be broken.

When the horse stumbles, you do not cut off its legs.

They cut his throat with a feather.

A low wall – anyone can leap over it.

A life of contemplation is better than the banners of war.

They asked the rabbit: why are you not a meat eater? It replied: I want to save my own skin.

He sees with his eyes, and covers with his tail.

Softer than the cheeks of a little girl.

If you want to be obeyed, order what can be done.

The one-eyed is king among the blind.

He who goes to the *ḥammām* will not come out absolutely clean.

There are two banks to every river.

Every horse will stumble at least once.

There is a defect in every beauty.

All that the virtuous woman needs is a cup and a jar.

Moustache (symbol of manly honour)

The brush tail of a fox

By my moustache!

Pledging one's honour.

May his moustache be shaved off.

If you hear they are shaving off your neighbour's moustache, start to pour water on yours.

From my veil to your moustache.

The bride's mother entrusting the bride's wellbeing to the groom's father.

Beware a man with a hairless face.

Neighbours

The value of a house is judged by its neighbours.

The neighbour before the house.

Your neighbour, your neighbour, your neighbour, then your brother.

Good morning, neighbour – you in your home, I in mine.

Treat your neighbour well even if he is bad.

Your neighbour has gone – now is the time to have your house repaired.

Notoriety

Arsenic, not lime.

> This alludes to the mixture of arsenic and lime used in the *ḥammām* for depilation. There is some debate as to whether the depilation is produced by the one material or the other.
>
> > Go relate to the Minister, if he would listen, a criticism
> > I see you in the *ḥammām* as lime
> > But it is His Excellency the adviser[47] who is the arsenic.

More notorious than the infidelity of Iblīs (Lucifer).

More famous than *qifā nabki.*

The opening words of the epic poem by Imru' al-Qays, one of the *mu'allaqāt* poems which were hung in the Ka'ba.

If you wish to win fame, commit an atrocity.

If you have to fight, do it at home.

Commit a sin on Friday, so you will be in the first row.

i.e. the first row in hell.

Pissing in the well of Zamzam.

The waters of the holy well outside Mecca, reputed to be the site of a miracle in the desert involving Hagar and her infant son Ismā'īl. One of the sites that are visited in the *ḥajj.*

Give me a hundred, but call me a desperado.

I do not mind you giving me 100 strokes of the lash as long as you acknowledge me as a desperado.

He would rather be in the front row of hell than among the slippers.

They beat the drum for him.

A reference to a public humiliation in which the victim is paraded in the streets on an ass, facing backwards, with the ass preceded by a drummer.

---

[47] A foreign political adviser.

They painted a flag for him.

> The parade on an ass may also be preceded, in addition to the drummer, by someone holding up a flag to attract attention.

Becoming a spectacle.

His wool is red.

> This is said of anyone who has become notorious for some bad character trait.

Obstinacy

A voice in his head.

He is his own Sultan.

He is beyond advice.

He put my advice behind his ear.

> i.e. ignored it.

He will not desist until a palm tree grows in his head, or the crow turns grey.

Nothing will make him dismount from his mule.

I tell him silk, he says felt.

I say 'A', he tells me 'B'.

His is the obstinacy of the beetle.

I shall wait for the cock to lay an egg before asking him again.

I shall light ten candles for him, and still not hope to change him.

Old age

He remembers the digging of the sea/river.

A contemporary of Noah.

He is older than *yakhnī.*

> *Yakhnī* is reputed to be the oldest dish known to man, the first to be prepared for Adam after he was expelled from paradise. It is said to have consisted of a stew of minced meat, chopped onion and lentils.

His foot is at the door of the grave.

When he reaches 60, prepare the knife for him.

The soul is green.

> It does not get old, unlike the body.

The aged lion is mocked by the jackals.

An old widower in the house is a burden, an old widow a bliss.

> Said of the latter, in particular, for looking after grandchildren.

His is the long age of the eagle.

His life span is measured by the rifle.

i.e. aiming at a distant target.

An old bear is the plaything of its cubs.

A Kashān.

The reference is to a superior Kāshān carpet, which becomes more valuable as it ages.

The beards have turned grey and they are still ignorant.

They circumcised him in his old age.

The worst time for the cock is when they wash its feet.

i.e. after it is slaughtered – the washing of feet is a funeral rite.

Parasite

A *laqqām*

An open mouth – lit. one who swallows one mouthful after another.

He hits the plate.

i.e. clears it of food.

A cat of the kitchen.

A thousand chickens in the belly of the fox.

A dog found a bone.

The wedding is for two people and two thousand gatecrashers.

He hitches his burden to his uncle's neck.

The whistle is your lad's, old woman.

> Anecdote: a man was going away to visit another country. Many people came to bid him farewell and to tell him what they wanted him to bring them back; but none offered to pay him except one old woman. She handed him a penny and asked him to get her a whistle for her grandson. He acknowledged her request by saying that she could take it that the whistle would certainly be forthcoming for her lad, since, unlike the others, she was paying for what she requested.

Patience

God is with the patient.

Patience is the key to relief.

What you may miss is just behind the door.

Because she (the cat) was in a hurry the kittens were born blind.

Continue to sit in the sun and wait for the shade.

Leave the honey in the pot and wait for the right price.

Greet your enemy in the morning and in the evening, keeping your feelings to yourself.

Do not throw the spear before the shabbūt.

> The shabbūt is a much-prized fish of the carp variety, found in the Tigris. Commonly caught by hook and line, it is also obtained by spearing. The point of the saying is that the fisherman was inclined to bring down the spear a fraction too soon.

Praiseworthiness

Melons of Samarra.

Pears of Isfahan.

As wholesome as *Kabar* (and see **Business** above).

Deserves a kiss on the forehead.

> Usually said of a young person's achievement.

No dead person is worth a lamentation.

The hand of the noble man is scales.

> In the past there was no uniformity in the scales and measures used by different tribes in Iraq, and no official weighbridges. Say a tribe agreed to sell an agreed quantity of wool to another, there would then be the question of how to go about weighing the goods to meet the term of the bargain and there would occasionally be an argument as to whether the scales used by one side or the other were

accurate. In such events it was not unknown for the parties to ask a trusted outsider to adjudicate, the latter verifying and making the adjustment, using his hand to feel the weight.

Profession

He who has a ladle does not burn his hand.

Go and acquire a profession, but it is to no avail without good luck.

Once you acquire a profession it is like a ring on your finger.

Begging is an alchemy.

Seven occupations, and all to no avail without good luck.

Be a draper who clothes them and a perfumier to make them smell sweet until your hair turns grey.

The master's apprentice is a master and a half.

Make yourself a mullā and put your trust in God.

The suggestion is that this is an easy profession.

Knowledge without deeds is like a rainless cloud.

Provocation

Pinching the bottom of Lucifer/the lion.

The kid ate the shepherd's pie.

Stealing the stick of the thief.

The pan by the fire, the man by words.

> Both boiling over.

Quandary

Between *Hāna* and *Māna* he lost his beard.

> Anecdote: there was a middle-aged man whose hair was turning grey. He had two wives: Hāna who was old, and Māna who was young. When he was with Hāna she would pick off the black hairs of his beard so that he would feel old. But when he was with Māna she would pick off the white hairs to make him feel young. That state of affairs continued until the husband lost his beard entirely.

A mouse that swallowed a bone.

Like someone who had swallowed a razor.

A head stuck in a hole.

A beetle enmeshed in wool.

Clover in thorn.

A ball of knitting wool lost its head.

Like the caprice of the goat.

To tie or untie (a load).

A date between two baskets.

An egg between two stones.

Like the dice in backgammon.

Having six faces, and thrown in the game of backgammon.

More complicated than the tail of the lizard.

Your policy, O Westerners, has become
wretched and bent like the lizard's tail
You are the reason for the outbreak of the war
you set it alight and it spread everywhere

They told him, divorce her and marry her sister. He replied, God's curse on the pair of them.

One cannot hold two pomegranates in one hand.

If you spit upwards it falls back on you, if you spit downwards it falls on your beard.

Like a mother who has lost her child.

Reconciliation

He took a share.

Listened to advice, and accepted it.

Enough, give it up and take a share
else you had better cut off your tongue
One cannot pinch the bottom of the lion

without thinking of the consequences

The cat weighs a stone and the meat a stone – why should we quarrel?

They said settle, we said settled.

Put the bitter at the bottom and the sweet on top.

The bad fruit is bad, the harvest is the harvest.

Nothing more to discuss.

Do not blame and you will not be blamed.

If he will not accept a share, add a lamb to the share.

If you are bitten by a dog, would you bite it back?

Take from the length and give from the width.

Let your adversary eat from the top as well as the bottom.

Treat the two banks equally, and Abū Ḥanīfa.

The two banks of the Tigris in Baghdad: the Kāẓumiyya, with its Shī'ī shrine, facing the A'ẓamiyya, with its Sunnī shrine of the great theologian Abū Ḥanīfa.

O noble angels, do us no harm and we will not harm you.

Said when moving house.

He who sees me with one eye, I will see with both of mine.

If he will not come towards me, I will go towards him.

Drink their water and be like them.

Resignation

Do not go chasing the wind that carried off your hat.

It was a bird, and it flew.

Your world, my friend, is like the winds.

> Accept it – there is no use in grieving.

Since you came, you might as well sit down.

> The Baghdadis attribute this saying to the people of Mosul as an example of their alleged meanness.

Better to sleep unhappy than to stay awake with regret.

What can I do? I have no blade.

Even gold bends on the anvil.

What is the milk's is the milk's, and what is the water's is the water's.

> The allusion is to the dishonest practice of adding water to milk intended for sale. The inference is that with the milk already diluted by the water there is nothing to be done about it.

Salvation

And will the taper be still burning at the break of dawn?

God will repair the tear in our drum.

No load will be left fallen on the road.

However long the sky remains overcast, God will still clear it.

Dead and resurrected.

Said of someone getting over a setback.

He snatched it from the lion's mouth.

Sarcasm

He butts with horns of mud.

Do you call this molasses, or is it mud?

A saw of a tongue.

i.e. a cutting tongue.

An ant bending the *malwiyya* of Samarra.[48]

He plants horns in the wilderness and hopes they will sprout as buffaloes.

How can you compare Ibn 'Abdaka with Murdokh and Shā'ul?

Ibn 'Abdaka was a celebrated Baghdadi 'noble outlaw' (an

Iraqi Robin Hood), who robbed the rich and (mostly) spared the poor. He operated in the Diyala province in the last days of Ottoman rule, at the end of the First World War. After the British occupation he joined the insurgency and featured in a dramatic event involving a raid on a train and the capture of the British Political Commissioner, Gertrude Bell. The comparison, said to be inappropriate, is with Murdokh, a Christian, and Shā'ul (Saul), a Jew.

He cursed the black grape.

A historical anecdote: the poet Ibn al-Qaba'tharī was with some friends in an orchard. The conversation turned to al-Hajjāj b. Yūsuf al-Thaqafī, the despotic and hated governor of Iraq. Ibn al-Qaba'tharī said, 'May Allāh blacken his face and cut off his head, and give me his blood to drink.' The remark was reported to al-Hajjāj, who had agents everywhere. He sent for al-Qaba'tharī and questioned him in the presence of an audience. 'What did you say about me?' 'Nothing,' replied the poet. 'Yes, you did,' retorted al-Hajjāj, 'you were in such and such a place and said, of me, Please, Allāh, blacken his face, cut off his head, and give me his blood to drink. Do you deny that you said those words?' 'I do not deny those words, O my Emir,' replied al-Qaba'tharī. 'I said them standing underneath a branch of black vine and I desired the juice of the fruit. But the fruit being still green I also expressed the desire that it matured and turned black before we could cut it off the branch.'

It is interesting to note that Ibn al-Qaba'tharī survived the ordeal. Al-Hajjāj would no doubt have seen through the subterfuge, but was content to accept it at face value in

---

[48] A massive and celebrated medieval monument.

public so as to save his face.

The fish starts to go off in the head.

A satirical political anecdote: a man came to buy a fish, and smelled its tail to see if it had gone off. The fishmonger, while assuring him that it was fresh, pointed out that if it had started to go bad, that would have started in the head. Replied the man: ‘I know that, but wanted to find out if the rottenness had got down as far as the tail.’

Every mule a gazelle in its mother’s eyes.

A thousand dogs do not make a gazelle.

Straight as a scythe!

The bald hen does not need a comb.

He who plants thorn will not harvest grape.

God giving walnuts to the toothless.

The fart of the camel is the amber of the beard.

And pointing specifically to the beard, that being on the same level as the camel’s posterior!

Safe is the bankrupt in the caravan.

Remaining estranged until the cock turns grey.

I did not say you will not be a governor – I said you will never be a man!

Anecdote, with an allusion to the Biblical story of Joseph in Egypt: a father upbraided his young son for his bad ways and told him, You will never be a man. The young man left home and went to another province where he did so well that he became its governor. He then ordered that his father be arrested and brought before him. This was done, the father not knowing the reason for the arrest and suffering humiliation and abuse on the way. Brought before his son the governor, the latter, preening himself, reminded his father of what he had said about him. The father responded with the above crushing statement.

The egg does not smash the stone.

All he needs is a horse and three horseshoes.

He having picked up one horseshoe on the road.

If a dog's prayer was answered, the sky would rain bones.

The *qursh* (a small Ottoman coin) spoke, and it was true; the tongue spoke and it was false.

Vinegar has become scarce in Basra.

Vinegar can be made with dates, and there are countless date trees in the Basra region.

They told the fox, How would you like to spend the night among the chickens? He said, I fear their pecking.

The moon is not affected by the barking of dogs.

Bāmia (okra) is like a gallstone in the mouth, and a calamity in the stomach.

The sea will not be soiled by the lick of a dog.

Between the truth and a lie is but the space of four fingers.

It is better to admit a thief to your house than a builder.

His smell knocks out the sparrow.

The smell is what you get at the door of the grave.

Self-reliance

In wings.

> Success through one's own efforts.

Every prophet prays for his own soul.

A drummer's feast (and see **Exaggeration**).

Use your own brain, for no one will lend you his.

Circumcise your son with an axe rather than having to rely on another.

The mule is his own guide.

> This also includes the implication that mules are preferred as beasts of burden.

Everyone is laid in one's own grave.

Do not weep for me, weep for yourself.

If the times are mistreating you, mistreat your arm.

> i.e. blame your indolence/shoddy work.

Like women at a lamentation, each one lamenting her own dead.

> The reference is to women at a Ḥusainī lamentation. The occasion is a lament of the martyrdom of Imām Husain which is transmuted by the women listeners to lamenting personal bereavements.

Better your own bread than a neighbour's cake.

He who counts on a neighbour's soup will go to bed hungry.

You only slake your thirst by holding the cup in your own hand.

Your fingers are best for scratching your back.

Cooked in its own fat!

Feed off your own arm so you won't need the butcher.

See with your own eyes, and cover your nakedness with your own tail.

Stupidity

Lying in the courtyard of the shrine.

> The allusion is to the old practice of laying a lunatic by a martyr's shrine.

Go and barter your brain for sweets.

Go and entrust fat to the cat.

He who does not plan will fall in the well.

He is like one carrying water in a tray.

The candle will not keep burning right up to the morning.

> This is a warning to the improvident (equivalent to saying that one spends as if there was no tomorrow).

Neither in his hand nor in his pocket.

> He has wasted all his money.

Reckless as a glass breaking as it strikes.

Those who gave us sermons have gone – we are left with those who shit.

He is as tall as the date palm, and his brains those of an ass.

> Among the Baghdadis extravagant height in a man is generally associated with simplicity and lack of guile (and see the next saying).

The tall man is an idiot, the short one seditious.

His skull is an empty *tank* (tin can).

> Anecdote: Ja‘far al-Ḥillāwī arrived late at a meeting, and found his friends sitting round a samovar of tea. While

they were waiting for him they had conspired to play a practical joke on him, by way of reproach for his lateness. So the host served tea to everyone in turn, except for Ja'far. The latter was acute enough to guess what they were up to; so he got up and left, but not before he composed some verses on a piece of paper which he left behind:

A samovar resembling the teat of a wet-nurse
  the lads of the quarter suckled in turn
Verily the samovar mirrored the brains of its owner
  both examined closely are *tanka* (tin can)

If the slave knew what will happen to him he would tear his clothes.

This is said of someone who is unobservant and absent-minded. There is also an implied evocation of the image of a sub-Saharan African slave tearing what little clothing he is dressed in.

They stuck a seal on his tail.

Comparing him to a stupid animal.

He butts the wall with his argument.

Implying a weak argument that gets nowhere.

So-and-so is ripe.

Blind labour.

Mismanagement.

He grinds garlic with his elbow.

A black crow.

Every one's madness is different.

He sold the vineyard to buy a winepress.

For want of faggots she burned the mat.

To the wise a hint, to the stupid a kick.

The bigger the beard, the smaller the brain.

Selling the house to pay for a manger.

Her child at her breast – and she's searching for it.

He who has no brain lives at ease.

Do you not know that they weave carpets in Kermanshah?

How did they catch you, O blackbird, you who claim to be careful?

Better blindness in the eyes than blindness in the brains.

The blame is the victim's, not the killer's.

The shepherd nodded, and the wolf got in among the sheep.

It doesn't cry, so it doesn't get suckled.

They offered the idiot a thousand brains, but he still preferred his own.

Let him loose among the gazelles and he will return with the oxen.

He seeks advice from oxen.

You might as well tether him by his ears.

Barefoot with henna, bald with flowers.

> The point of the saying is that it would make more sense to wear shoes than to smear one's feet with henna, and more seemly to cover one's bald pate than to be visiting with a bunch of flowers.

His wheat eats his barley.

> Inferring bad husbandry.

Hoping to get honey from the wasp.

When he falls in the well the first time, he's a martyr; when he falls in a second time, he's an idiot.

He is like an absent-minded prophet.

Our governor is a child; woe to the people.

Like the donkey that can only see what's between its front legs.

An ass when he talks, a wall when he keeps quiet.

Superstition

Whose face in the morning?

> The belief that the first person that you see in the morning will either bring you good luck or ill fortune.

The owl of the ruins.

> Thought to presage disaster.

The crow of separation.

> Presaging the break up of lovers.

Watering the good angels in the soil.

> When a person is about to set out on a long or hazardous journey, his closest relative will follow him to the street door with a tumbler full of water, the contents of which, for good luck, are flung in the wake of the person departing.

Sell the first house, let the second and live in the third.

'atbat khayr (a lucky threshold).

From the soothsayer to the astrologer.

Learn your fortune from the mouth of a child.

Most of the victims in the graves were undone by 'the (evil) eye'.

Do not show your bread to the hungry.

A stick in the eye for him who envies.

An incantation against the evil eye.

The cherry is the sweeper of prosperity.

Some people consider the cherry tree unlucky. This is based on the fact that it fruits at the end of the (fruiting) season.

No one knows which pip carries the blessing.

That is based on the belief that one of the pips of the pomegranate is heavenly.

Sneezing is a guard against madness.

He who sneezes will live.

This refers specifically to a newborn baby or to someone on his/her deathbed.

The table (and table manners)

Eat like the camel, and rise with the others.

That is a Bedouin saying. People dine in groups – one group after another, according to their social station. As one group finishes it is followed by the next. If one of a group has had enough he should still wait, and rise at the same time as the rest of his group. Hence, a big eater should eat rapidly (as does the camel), but wait for the others to finish.

He who kills a snake should eat it.

> This is based on the belief that to settle food in the stomach one should 'kill' it by adding a drink of tea or coffee – hence, the dinner can be followed by the suggestion, How about eating the snake?

Rather waste your money than waste your teeth.

The lemon cures the fat.

> This is based on the belief that the juice of the lemon counteracts the fattiness of meat. The expression is said by way of encouraging the guest to consume the rich food on offer.

The delight is in the hot, the blessing in the cold.

> This is said in praise of the salad and the fruit.

Shed my blood and give me a mouthful of rice.

Without dates there would have been no Arab nation.

> The implication is that one desires dates so much that it is very death to be deprived of them; Also an acknowledgment of their abundance in Arab countries – Iraq in particular.

Eating to the extent of the friendship.

> That is said by the host to encourage the guest to eat, on the basis that the amount to be consumed would be commensurate with the warmth of the friendship.

That is a gift in common.

This is said humorously by boon companions just as a gift of food is received by their host, thereby claiming to share it.

In good health!

This would be exclaimed at hearing a diner belching, which is taken to be a sign of satisfaction, and, in Bedouin society, not considered impolite.

Teaching

You don't teach the orphan how to weep.

You don't teach the singer how to sing.

You do not teach the fox how to eat chickens.

He who teaches me a word shall own me as his slave.

You take the flesh and leave me the bones.

This is said by the father of a new pupil, addressing the teacher and urging him to beat learning and good manners into his new charge.

Thrift

The white *qirsh*[49] will be useful in the dark days.

Pāra by *pāra* and the tin will fill up.

A variant: Drop by drop and the jar will fill up.

Grain by grain and there'll be enough for the pie.

[49] *Qirsh* and *pāra* were small value Ottoman coins.

Treachery

Under the *'abāya* (cloak).

They soaped the floor before you, O old man.

Straw covering water.

The times are digging you a well.

They laid thorn in my path, knowing I was barefoot.

A rope made of *wabar.*

Camel hair, deceptively strong.

Everyone of them a traitor, soft and tough
like the proverbial *wabar* rope

The guardian is the thief.

The heart of a wolf and the face of a sheep.

A warden turned thief.

A boot for the scorpion.

How many Solomons are undone by Solomon!

Uncertainty

God often intervenes between the morsel and the mouth.

God gives you one thing and takes away another.

Foundations of sand.

Foundations of water.

Fish in the sea.

Vicissitudes

The world has become a Ferris wheel taking us up and down.

When straight it's a knife, when curved a scythe.

What falls from the sky is bound to hit the earth.

The moon doesn't last even for one month.

It didn't endure, even for the Prophet.

The Times are like the water of the *narghile*.

i.e. in turmoil; going up and down.

Time is high tide and low tide.

One day for you, one day against you.

Time has become the enemy of the worthy, while it befriends the base.

Time has befriended the vile five to five.

A handshake.

Time takes your dīnār and gives you half a dirham back.

From one hour to the next a thousand turbans may topple.

Rubble has replaced the bricks.

One hour easterly, the next westerly.

> The easterly wind in Baghdad brings rain, the westerly brings cool air and clear skies.

A noble saddle is put on the ass, and rags on the steed.

They shod the beetle in slippers of gold.

The tail is now the head, the head the tail.

The son of the tall woman has become short, and the son of the small woman tall.

Broken is my sickle.

Gone the ‘Īd and its joys, everyone back to rags!

The prices of onions and garlic have now gone up while that of the pear of Isfahan is down.

I was silver, now I’m coal.

We were the owners of the house, now we are mere guests.

Teak to finish[50].

---

[50] ”Teak” is Persian for “good”, “finish” is derived from the English to mean “bad”.

Weather

February is the tail end of the grapes and figs.

February isn't over yet – it's not the time to frolic.

There are no rules in February.

February doesn't keep its word.

February is the enemy of old women.

Fire is the fruit of winter.

Keep a store of coal in March.

Flaming August lifts the nail from the door.

> Variant: The first ten of August burn off the nail in the door
> The second ten of August lessen the dates in the trees
> The third ten of August open the door ajar to winter
> The fourth ten of August open the door of hell

August empties the cup of its water.

Sun that burns the sparrow's head.

September, a lot of wheat and a lot of cucumber.

Beware the rains of September.

Go and die, O ass, until the spring comes.

The sky will not remain overcast for ever.

Summer is the father of the poor.

Well-being

He has the whole world in his box.

He's wealthy and the date trees are loaded.

Wealth covers all faults.

Silk goes with everything.

The apples in the grove are cheek by jowl.

He carries a gallstone and an amulet.

A double guard (belt and braces) against the evil eye.

An old slipper is hung outside his door.

To ward off envy.

The fortunate woman sits on a sofa.

His rope is a cord.

Using the superior cord for rope

His bread is underneath the bowl.

His wealth is inherited.

He toys with a lira as if it were a fils.

The lira is a high-value coin; the fils is the smallest coin, one thousand to a dīnār.

The morsel reached his mouth.

Fussclass.

First class.

Wisdom

He who is one day older than you is a whole year wiser (see **Experience**).

A wise man hears the soft fart of the ant.

A wise man buys and does not sell.

i.e. listens and says nothing.

His eyes remain open even as he is immersed in *leben* (liquid yoghurt).

Connoting vigilance.

If you don't push it with a bamboo cane now, you'll need to use a pole later on.

Better be a hammer than an anvil.

The snake knows its killer.

A wise enemy is better than a foolish friend.

> A fable: a man had a lion for a faithful companion. Every time the man slept the lion stood guard over him. One day the man was fast asleep under a tree when a bee landed on his face, which the lion pawed away. The bee landed again and once more the lion pawed it away. After the third occasion, fearing that his friend's sleep was being disturbed, and wanting to get rid of the bee for good, the lion picked up a boulder and held it up waiting to see what the bee would do. As the bee landed on the face of the man the lion brought down the boulder with all his might, killing his friend.

An intelligent guess is better than a stupid fact.

He can read what had been rubbed out.

You will not lead a raft past a wise man.

To be superstitious is to be wise.

A live ass is better than a dead philosopher.

Perhaps a wise word from the mouth of a fool.

Three things the wise don't talk about: the journey before it ends; the war before it's won, and a new child before it's delivered.

For want of a wise man, put on a turban and advise.

He who does not guard his estate like a man will lose it like a woman.

We listened to his talk and belched.

Felt replete; heard all we wanted to hear.

The flesh of the sages is indigestible.

Knowledge without action is like a rainless cloud.

Every commodity goes up in price when scarce – except wisdom.

You do not see God with your eyes; you will know him with your brain.

There is no shame in asking for advice/a direction.

Consult your elders, discuss it with those younger than you, then go back to do what you were minded to do.

The gap between the wise and the fool may be a single hair, yet it will not break.

The wise man does not fly his flock of birds when it is foggy.

This refers to the Baghdadi urban sport of flying one's flock of pigeons from the roof, the point being to inveigle a pigeon from a rival's flock to be disorientated, separated from its flock and captured as it joins the one's own.

The wise man knows the period of gestation.

Hence, whose child it is.

Hang the question on the neck of the wise, and feel safe.

Carry it before you rest, and lay it down before you get exhausted.

Don't say it's sesame, until you taste it in your mouth.

The wisest answer: I don't know.

Women

Women are grass roots.

Bringing about social networking and alliances through marriage.

Women are the army of Satan.

Whoever marries mother, him will I call uncle/sir.

I told her, I divorce you – she said, come to bed.

Every man with two wives is a *ḥammāl* (carrier/beast of burden),

God's curse is on the hairy woman and a smooth man.

Better live as a cock for one day than a hundred years as a woman.

Zanāna (Persian for woman).

Commonly used to refer to an effeminate man.

With his munificence she gets others.

The reference is to a rich man's widow.

Better a mad son than a lady for a daughter.

Better daughters than being barren.

The daughter is a door knocker.

Responds to every suitor.

Three things for a good life: a big house, a speedy horse and an obedient wife.

A variant: the seven virtues of a wife are: being honourable, a good mother, a good manager, being contented, loving her husband, showing good manners towards friends and neighbours, a good keeper of confidences.

She combs my grey hair and washes my '*abāya* – that's enough for me.

Consult them and then go against their advice.

The husband needs seven blessings in his wife; the wife needs only one.

To be loved.

My only lovers are a dog and an ignoramus.

Said by a woman.

The monkey is a gazelle in its mother's eyes

The eye and what it sees, the heart and what it desires.

Written on the door of Paradise: a mother-in-law hates Paradise.

If daughter-in-law and mother-in-law loved each other, heaven would be crowded with women.

Variant: A woman who loves her daughter-in-law opens the door of heaven even to Iblīs (Lucifer).

If the moon is with me what do I care for the stars?

As long as my husband is on my side I do not care about his relatives.

The wife brings her prosperity with her.

Addressed to a would-be husband by way of encouragement.

Marry an honourable woman and sleep without suspicion.

Choose the mother before the daughter.

Some soap, and a slave woman is a lady.

The fat covers the foibles.

This is said in praise of a well-built woman.

She asks the moon to go into eclipse so she will shine in its place.

Her slippers on the doorstep and her '*abāya* on the coat hook.

Ever ready to go out shopping.

Sixty women over a blue shard.

Competing in the market to buy a trifle.

If you want to humiliate a man give him a wife; if you want to vex a woman give her a child.

Wash your son's face – you do not know who may kiss it; wash your house – you do not know who may visit.

A thousand leaves and not the tree.

> Rather lose the children than the husband.

Your mother, your mother, then your father.

Not every woman in a face mask can claim to be free.

> A historical reference: with the arrival in Iraq of so many girl slaves in the early Abbasid period (ninth century AD) it became the norm for free women to cover their faces, while it was forbidden for female slaves to do so (except in special cases).

They said 'white' and stopped; they said 'dark' and explained.

> This illustrates the favouring of a white and fresh complexion. In describing a potential bride the matchmaker need say no more than that the girl is white to define her looks. But in the case of a dark complexion there is a need to expound further on the girl's appearance, including the fact that there are so many shades of 'dark'.

The first glance a pleasure, the second adultery.

Women leave their intelligence at home.

> That is, when they go out shopping.

Lightning Source UK Ltd.
Milton Keynes UK
UKOW06f0356141117
312689UK00005B/398/P

9 781780 881584